409A:

The 100 Most Frequently Asked Questions

Brian W. Berglund • Louis R. Richey

American Law Institute
American Bar Association
Continuing Professional Education

Board of Directors

4025 Chestnut Street, Philadelphia, Pennsylvania 19104-3099 • www.ali-aba.org

409A:

The 100 Most Frequently Asked Questions

Brian W. Berglund, Bryan Cave LLP
Louis R. Richey, JD, SRVP, McCamish Systems LLC, an Infosys Company

·025 Chestnut Street | Philadelphia, Pennsylvania 19104-2899
ʼww.ali-aba.org

Library of Congress Control Number: 2010915331

Printed in the United States of America

ISBN: 9780831899752

Second Printing 2011

John B. Spitzer of the ALI-ABA staff
supervised the production of this book.

ALI-ABA has a history of outreach to underrepresented groups in the legal community and is firmly committed to providing a welcoming environment and ensuring that the attorneys who speak and write for our organization represent the increasing diversity of our profession. We welcome suggestions for new speakers and authors, especially from underrepresented groups in the legal community, to support the full participation of all of the talent in our profession.

Nothing in this publication should be considered as the rendering of legal advice. Non-lawyers should seek the advice of a licensed attorney in all legal matters. Readers should assure themselves that the material in this publication is still current and applicable at the time it is read. Neither ALI-ABA nor the author can warrant that the material will continue to be accurate, nor do they warrant it to be completely free of errors when published. Readers should verify statements before relying on them. The materials in this publication reflect the viewpoints of the author and do not necessarily express the opinions of ALI-ABA Continuing Professional Education or its sponsors.

About the Authors

Brian W. Berglund, Bryan Cave LLP

Mr. Berglund is a partner in the St. Louis, Missouri, office of Bryan Cave LLP, an international law firm. Mr. Berglund has spent his entire legal career with Bryan Cave, encompassing almost 30 years. He is a member of the firm's Employee Benefits and Executive Compensation Group and its Tax Advice & Controversy Group. He primarily represents large employers with sophisticated plans. He routinely counsels clients on tax law (especially with regard to Code Section 409A), ERISA, securities laws and other issues relating to the design and structure of most types of executive and employee benefit plans, including appropriate structures for employment agreements, severance plans, stock options plans, nonqualified deferred compensation plans, qualified plans, cafeteria and fringe benefit, and other welfare benefit plans. Mr. Berglund is listed in "The Best Lawyers in America" and "Missouri/Kansas Super Lawyers," and is a Fellow in the American College of Employee Benefits Counsel.

Mr. Berglund graduated magna cum laude and Phi Beta Kappa with a degree in mathematics from Carleton College in Minnesota, and graduated Order of the Coif from the Washington University School of Law in St. Louis. He was an adjunct professor of law at the Washington University School of Law for five years, where he taught a three-hour course in the graduate tax program entitled, "Advanced Topics in Employee Benefits." He has served as President of the Employee Benefits Association of St. Louis, Missouri.

In addition to teaching, Mr. Berglund frequently lectures on executive and employee benefits and tax-related topics and issues to various law and bar groups. He has spoken regularly for ALI-ABA programs and programs covering executive and employee benefits, as well as St. Louis and Missouri Bar Association events and programs. His most recent speaking appearance on Code Section 409A, entitled "Section 409A Corrections Program," occurred in March 2009 at a St. Louis Metropolitan Bar Association event.

Mr. Berglund is also a published author. His articles have appeared in a number of ALI-ABA program materials, the *Employment Law Journal, Corporate Law Counselor*, and *St. Louis Bar Association Journal*, among others. His most recent article on Code Section 409A, entitled, "Correcting 409A Violations to Minimize Deferred Compensation Taxes," appeared in the *St. Louis Bar Association Journal* in the winter 2009 edition.

Mr. Berglund can be reached at bwberglund@bryancave.com.

Louis R. Richey, JD, SRVP, McCamish Systems LLC, an Infosys Company

Mr. Richey is an attorney by training and currently Senior Vice President with McCamish Systems LLC, an Infosys Company located in Atlanta, Georgia. McCamish Systems is one of the nation's leading providers of outsourced administrative and other back-office support services for life insurance carriers and other major financial services organizations, such as banks and brokerage companies. Infosys is a leading global IT and administration BPO company. Mr. Richey helps lead the McCamish Retirement Services Group.

Mr. Richey is the legal and content expert for all of McCamish's executive, employee and qualified and nonqualified pension benefit Web-based marketing, design and plan administration platforms (McCamish is the largest nonqualified plan TPA in the US today, based on the recordkeeping assets report of its clients in a late 2009 PlanSponsor study). However, he is widely known as a financial and executive benefits products and services marketing innovator, and author. He is also recognized as an experienced executive and employee benefits attorney, with special expertise on 409A nonqualified deferred compensation plans and other retirement plans, with over 30 years' experience in executive and employee benefits compensation consulting, planning and insurance for Fortune 1000 public, closely held and tax-exempt organizations and their employees. At earlier points in his career, Mr. Richey served as a senior marketing officer, or technical compensation and senior consultant, with employers such as American Express Company, the General American Life Insurance Company, William M. Mercer, Magner Network and several offices of the Management Compensation Group (MCG) and M Group.

He is a graduate of Wabash College in Indiana, a cum laude graduate of the Indiana University Law School in Indianapolis, and a member of the Indiana and Georgia Bars as well as the Federal Bar. He is currently a member of the BNA and National Underwriter Editorial Advisory Boards. He is also a retired Chairman of the Board of Visitors of the Indiana University Law School, Indianapolis. He has been named a Kentucky Colonel and an Arkansas Traveler in recognition of his professional contributions to the legal profession.

Mr. Richey lectures widely on the impact and implications of Code Section 409A, executive and employee benefit topics, retirement planning, financial services marketing, insurance, and financial planning, including major conferences and institutes such as the New York University Federal Tax Institute (2×), Southwest Federal Tax Conference, Notre Dame Estate Planning Institute, the American Society of Actuaries Annual Conference, the LIMRA Advance Marketing Conference, LIMRA/LOMA Conference, KnowledgeCongress, and a host of other financial industry webinars, conferences and meetings.

Mr. Richey's comments have appeared in *Business Week, The Wall Street Journal, Forbes*, and *Investor's Daily*, and he has appeared on the Financial News Network for National Public Radio. He has authored or co-authored a number of books and BNA portfolios, plus more than 300 articles, audios and videos on compensation and tax topics.

Mr. Richey is widely known for helpful practice-oriented books, including *The 409A Nonqualified Deferred Compensation Advisor (Covered & Exempt Plans Under 409A)*, 5th Edition, which is available from the National Underwriter Company; and BNA Tax Management Portfolios #386 4th, and #282 2nd, entitled, "Compensating Employees with Life Insurance."

In the past 24 months, Mr. Richey has since authored or co-authored five major articles on 409A and nonqualified deferred compensation plans, and also one on Code Section 101(j) requirements governing employer-owned life insurance (EOLI), frequently used as employer assets behind plans. In the 1980s, the Internal Revenue Service even used one of his published articles in training materials for its own estate and gift tax agents and attorneys.

Mr. Richey can be reached at LRichey@McCamish.com

We have long had death and taxes as the two standards of inevitability. But there are those who believe that death is the preferable of the two. "At least," as one man said, "there's one advantage about death; it doesn't get worse every time Congress meets."

--Erwin N. Griswold

You must pay taxes. But there's no law that says you gotta leave a tip.

--Morgan Stanley
(advertisement)

Introduction

Code Section 409A is an astonishing tax provision. Its punitive taxes will only be imposed if someone makes a mistake. Because the rules associated with Section 409A are so complex, however, Section 409A compliance mistakes are almost inevitable.

When Code Section 409A was enacted in late 2004 (to become effective as to accruals earned or vested under "nonqualified deferred compensation plans" on and after January 1, 2005), the scope of the new Code section enacted in response to some select abuses occasioned by several high-profile corporate bankruptcies was not widely recognized. In the four years of the new Code section's transition period since the effective date, the breadth of the definition of "nonqualified deferred compensation plans" and the full impact of Code Section 409A have become evident. Code Section 409A has arguably become the single most expansive (and therefore important) Code section applicable to compensation and benefits since the beginning of the Code itself. As of January 1, 2009, the official end of the transition period, Code Section 409A now requires "actual" (rather than "good faith") documentary and operational compliance.

In general, it is now recognized that the reach of Code Section 409A is so broad that compensation and benefit practitioners should initially regard any compensation and benefit "arrangement" (to use Section 409A language) as potentially subject to Code Section 409A's documentary and operational requirements until the practitioner is satisfied that a statutory or regulatory exception from 409A coverage applies. The penalties for failure to comply with Code Section 409A are so severe (immediate income inclusion on deferred amounts as well as a 20% additional tax and interest penalty on such amounts) that a practitioner cannot afford to do otherwise for his or her client. Moreover, Section 409A can apply to arrangements even for a single individual, and regardless of the individual's level in the organization.

Section 409A itself is remarkably concise, covering only a couple of pages in the Internal Revenue Code. Official guidance issued to date, however, is extensive, covering literally hundreds of pages in the form of proposed and final regulations, extensive preambles explaining the proposed and final regulations, notices, and announcements. Moreover, additional guidance is expected soon. Some of the most important questions are not explicitly addressed in the official guidance, but have been answered by the drafters of the regulations during speeches and presentations. In general, the Internal Revenue Service and Treasury have taken the point of view that service providers and/or service recipients must be prevented from manipulating the rules to evade Congressional intent, and the detailed guidance to date reflects this wary attitude. Despite this detailed guidance – or perhaps because of it – even experienced practitioners disagree regarding the answers to some of the most basic compliance questions arising out of Section 409A.

As a consequence of these factors, and because of the broad range of questions generated by Code Section 409A, the demand for user-friendly assistance in accessing and navigating the official and unofficial guidance thus far issued has been intense. In their separate but complementary practices and businesses (one author as a practicing employee benefits attorney for a major law firm and the second as the internal legal support for one of the largest 409A plan administration organizations in the USA), the authors are confronted daily by the many and varied Code Section 409A documentation and operational questions, many of which are of first impression. Like other practitioners, we, the authors, recognize the need for a quick access and summary answer Code Section 409A resource. Out of that process grew this publication summarizing the answers to questions that we found were most frequently asked (or we had to ask ourselves to revise an existing arrangement, draft a new arrangement, or properly administer a new or grandfathered plan) during the past five and one-half years since enactment of Code Section 409A.

In addition, not only are the 100 most frequently asked questions on Code Section 409A and their answers summarized in this publication, but also each question includes citations to the current authority for the answer, including the law, the proposed and final regulations and IRS formal and informal guidance. This enables the practitioner quick access to the Code Section 409A source material behind each answer to permit further detailed research on the more complex Code Section 409A questions that we know from experience frequently arise in day-to-day practice.

We recognize that this first edition pertaining to Code Section 409A does not encompass all the questions and answers relating to the application of Code Section 409A. However, we believe that the practitioner will find that this publication is a useful and helpful start. We hope that practitioners will share both their desires and needs from this publication with us, based on their everyday use of it, so that planned future editions will be increasingly more useful. We are certain that at some point, there will be more than 100 questions in future editions, and this publication will become "Code Section 409A – Frequently Asked Questions." In the meantime, feel free to contact us at BWBerglund@BryanCave.com (Brian W. Berglund) and LRichey@McCamish.com (Louis R. Richey) if we can answer any questions about the publication or its content.

B.W.B., L.R.R.

Contents

Table Of Contents

PLANS SUBJECT TO SECTION 409A

Q.1. What types of compensation and benefit plans are subject to Section 409A?

Anyone hoping to find a clear definition of exactly what types of compensation are subject to Section 409A of the Internal Revenue Code of 1986 ("Code") will be disappointed. As more fully explained in Question 3, the Section 409A regulations start with the proposition that almost every type of compensation arrangement constitutes a "deferral of compensation" potentially subject to Section 409A, but then set forth a series of exceptions and exclusions from the application of Section 409A with respect to specific categories of compensation. This construct requires that a practitioner begin with the general assumption that the compensation in question is subject to Section 409A and then determine whether an exception or exclusion applies.

Under the regulations, a deferred compensation plan can encompass any compensation arrangement, whether written or oral, including an arrangement for one individual. Moreover, compensation that may be subject to a contingency or other vesting conditions may be subject to Section 409A. As long as there is a promise – even a contingent promise – to pay compensation in a future taxable year, a Section 409A issue arises that must be further analyzed.

The legal form and purpose of the recipient of the services are not material. The service recipient can be an individual, partnership, corporation or any variation of those forms; it can be for-profit or not-for-profit, taxable or tax-exempt. (See **Q. 6.**)

The provider of the services can be an employee of an employer, a director of a corporation, a partner of a partnership, an unrelated independent contractor, or a cash-basis corporation or personal service organization. (See **Q. 7.**)

Because nonqualified deferred compensation is defined so broadly under the Section 409A regulations, but then made subject to numerous exceptions, it is difficult to list all of the plans or arrangements that may potentially be subject to Section 409A. Having said this, the following types of plans, which have historically been commonly denominated as nonqualified deferred compensation plans, are almost always subject to Section 409A:

- Unfunded participant account balance plans (nonqualified defined contribution plans based on participant elective deferrals)

- Unfunded employer account balance plans (nonqualified defined contribution matching plans, employer awards of additional deferred compensation under nonqualified defined contribution plans)

- Unfunded employer non-account balance plans (nonqualified defined benefit plans)

The following plans or arrangements have not historically been considered to constitute nonqualified deferred compensation but may, under certain circumstances, be subject to Section 409A unless structured to fit within an exception or exclusion:

- Equity plans (stock option plans, stock appreciation rights)

- Split-dollar life insurance plans

- Severance and separation pay plans

- Post-employment reimbursement and fringe benefit plans

- Change in control plans

- Bonus plans

- Foreign plans

Deferred compensation arrangements potentially subject to Section 409A are frequently embedded in employment agreements, employment letters, commission arrangements, bonus arrangements, Code Section 457(f) top-hat plans sponsored by Code Section 501(c)(3) organizations, post-employment medical reimbursement arrangements, and partnership plans.

Citation: *See generally* 26 USC Section 409A(d); Treasury Regulation Section 1.409A-1(a)-(b).

Q.2. What plans are not subject to Section 409A?

The following specific exceptions are stated in the statute and regulations.

Statutory Exceptions:

- Tax-qualified employer retirement plans that satisfy the requirements of Code Section 401(a) (*e.g.*, 401(k) plans, defined benefit pension plans and ESOPs)

- Simple retirement plans described in Code Section 408(p) or simplified employee pension plans (sometimes referred to as SEPs) described in Code Section 408(k)

- Tax-deferred annuities that satisfy the requirements of Code Section 403(b)

- Eligible plans maintained by governmental and tax-exempt Section 501(c)(3) entities that satisfy the requirements of Code Section 457(b)

- Bona fide vacation, leave, disability pay (**Q. 10**), compensatory time and death benefit plans (most split-dollar life insurance plans do not fit within this exception as explained more fully in Question 79)
- Code Section 223 health savings accounts, Code Section 220 "Archer" medical savings accounts, flexible spending accounts and certain other medical reimbursement arrangements

Regulatory Exceptions:

- Short-term deferrals (**Q. 17**)
- Equity plans that meet the requirements of Code Sections 422 (incentive stock options) and 423 (employee stock purchase plans) (**Q. 73**)
- Nonqualified stock options and stock appreciation rights (a) that have a strike price no less than fair market value on the date of grant and (b) that meet certain other requirements (**Q. 69**)
- Non-collectively bargained severance plans that provide benefits for involuntary separation, separation for good reason or separation during limited window periods, with limits on the amount payable and the period of payment (**Q. 61**)
- Collectively bargained severance plans (**Q. 68**)
- Non-taxable benefits under Code Sections 104-106 (medical, dental, vision), 117 (tuition benefits), 119 (meals and lodging), 127 (educational assistance programs), 129 (dependent care assistance benefits) and 132 (certain fringe benefits) (**Q. 76**)
- Taxable education benefits (*e.g.*, books, tuitions, and fees) for courses other than those involving sports, games, or hobbies.
- Endorsement and bona fide loan split-dollar arrangements (**Q. 79**)
- Teacher employment contracts that permit payment of compensation over 12 months rather than the 9- or 10-month school year during which it is earned (**Q. 53**)
- Certain indemnification and liability insurance agreements (**Q. 78**)
- Certain legal settlement agreements between the service recipient and the service provider (**Q. 78**)
- Normal end-of-period payroll overlapping two tax years (**Q. 16**)
- Section 83 restricted property transfers (**Q. 74**)
- Foreign plans that satisfy an otherwise applicable exception or that cover only non-resident aliens with no United States source income (**Q. 83**)
- Arrangements between accrual method taxpayers (**Q. 7**)

- Deferred compensation to independent contractors serving multiple non-affiliated service recipients (**Q. 7**)

Citation: ***See generally*** **26 USC Section 409A(d); Treasury Regulation Section 1.409A-1(a)-(b).**

Q.3. What constitutes a deferral of compensation for purposes of Section 409A?

For purposes of Section 409A, a deferral of compensation occurs if and when, under the terms of the agreement and the relevant facts and circumstances, the plan participant acquires a legally binding right in one year to receive compensation that is or may be due and payable in a later year.

A substantial risk of forfeiture does not diminish a payee's legally binding right to deferred compensation for this purpose.

However, no deferral of compensation occurs if the service provider has unilateral unqualified discretion to reduce or eliminate the compensation after the services have been performed, unless it is unlikely that the service provider will ever exercise this right or the service provider's exercise of the right is tied to objective criteria.

The only types of compensation that will not fit within this extremely broad definition are compensation that must be paid in the calendar year in which the legally binding right to compensation arises and compensation that is subject to the sole discretion of the employer or other service recipient. (See **Q. 5**.) For example, if an employer advises an employee that the employer may pay the employee a bonus sometime in the future in the sole and absolute discretion of the employer, subject to completely subjective criteria, such that the employee will have no legal recourse whatsoever if the employer chooses not to pay a bonus, then the discretionary bonus would generally not fall within the definition of deferred compensation.

Note the breadth of this general definition. It potentially includes virtually any type of compensation that an employer or other service recipient has a contractual obligation to pay, including an obligation subject to satisfaction of future conditions. Even base pay may, in certain circumstances, be considered to constitute a deferral of compensation under this definition. For example, assume an employee renders services to an employer in late December 2010 and, as is typical, will not receive payment for those services until the end of the first pay period in January 2011. Under the general definition described above, a deferral of compensation has occurred because the employee has a legally binding right during 2010 to compensation that will be payable in a later taxable year, 2011. However, this pay pattern falls within an exception to the general definition of deferred compensation applicable to amounts paid shortly after they are earned pursuant to customary payroll practices. (See **Q. 16**.)

Payments that are considered short-term deferrals (**Q. 17**) also fall within an exception to this broad definition and therefore are not considered to constitute a deferral of compensation.

Citation: 26 USC Section 409A(d)(1); Treasury Regulation Section 1.409A-1(b).

Q.4. When is it determined whether a plan is subject to Section 409A?

This determination is made when the participant obtains a legally binding right to the deferred compensation. A plan generally becomes binding when it is no longer subject to reduction in benefits or termination by the unilateral act of the service recipient. (See **Q. 5.**)

Citation: Treasury Regulation Section 1.409A-1(c)(3).

Q.5. When is a plan legally binding for purposes of Section 409A?

A service provider does not have a legally binding right to compensation under a plan to the extent that the compensation may be unilaterally reduced or eliminated by the service recipient. However, if the facts and circumstances suggest that that the right to reduce or eliminate compensation lacks substantial significance or is available or exercisable only upon a condition, then the right to deferred compensation is treated as legally binding. In general, there is no substantial significance to a power to reduce or eliminate a service provider's right to deferred compensation if the service provider (i) has effective control over the person retaining the discretion; (ii) has effective control over any part of the compensation of the person retaining the discretion; or (iii) is a member of the family of the person retaining discretion (determined under Code Section 267(c)(4), applied as if the family also includes the spouse of any family member). There is no unilateral power to reduce or eliminate compensation if the criteria for reduction or elimination are by operation of the plan's terms (although this could qualify as a Section 409A substantial risk of forfeiture). Finally, the employer has a legally binding obligation under a plan (typically an excess plan) even if the plan's benefit formula provides for offset by tax-qualified plan benefits or benefits are reduced by actual or notional losses or subsequent decreases in compensation used to calculate final average compensation.

Citation: Treasury Regulation Section 1.409A-1(b)(1).

Q.6. Who is the service recipient for purposes of Section 409A?

The service recipient is an individual or any type of legal entity that is the recipient of services rendered in exchange for a legally binding commitment to pay deferred compensation.

The legal form and purpose of the recipient of the services are not material. The recipient can be an individual, partnership, corporation or any variation of those forms; it can be for-profit or not-for-profit, taxable or tax-exempt. The service recipient includes all entities treated as a single employer with the service recipient for purposes of Code Section 414(b) or (c). For example, if an employee provides services to the ABC Corporation, then the service recipient is considered to include not only the ABC Corporation, but also all entities aggregated with the ABC Corporation as a single employer under Code Sections 414(b) and (c). If the parent of the ABC Corporation were to provide a nonqualified deferred compensation plan for the benefit of the employee, then Section 409A would apply to that plan even though the payment of the compensation is not made by the ABC Corporation but by its parent.

Note that in the context of nonqualified stock options and stock appreciation rights, the Section 414(b) and (c) aggregation rules are applied to determine whether stock constitutes service recipient stock, except that as little as a 20% interest can be considered a controlling interest for purposes of these aggregation rules. (See **Q. 70.**)

Citation: Treasury Regulation Section 1.409A-1(g).

Q.7. Who is the service provider for purposes of Section 409A?

The provider of the services can be an employee of an employer, a director of a corporation, a partner of a partnership or an unrelated independent contractor. A service provider may also be a cash basis corporation, partnership or personal service organization. Accrual basis service providers are not subject to Section 409A.

An independent contractor who is actively engaged in providing services with respect to a trade or business other than as a board of directors member is exempt from Section 409A if the independent contractor provides "significant services" to two or more unrelated service recipients. Whether an independent contractor is providing significant services to two or more unrelated service recipients depends on the facts and circumstances. A safe harbor exists in the situation in which the independent contractor earns 70% or less of his or her income from any one such service recipient over the prior three years.

Citation: Treasury Regulation Section 1.409A-1(f).

Q.8. Are compensation and benefit plans of tax-exempt organizations subject to Section 409A?

Generally, yes. The same exceptions also apply. (See **Q. 2.**) Note in particular that Section 457(b) plans are exempt from Section 409A. Plans governed by Code Section 457(f) (*i.e.*, plans that do not meet the requirements for favorable tax treatment under Section 457(b)) are subject to both Code Section 457(f) and potentially Section 409A, unless an exception applies. Often the short-term deferral exception will apply, since Section 457(f) plans usually involve compensation subject to a substantial risk of forfeiture.

Note: Substantial risk of forfeiture has been defined differently for purposes of Section 409A and Section 83, which governs the tax treatment of property transfers in exchange for services. Prior to the enactment of Section 409A, the IRS had applied the definition set forth in Section 83 for purposes of Section 457(f), but the IRS has adopted a narrower definition in the regulations governing Section 409A. The IRS has suggested that the Section 409A definition also be applied for purposes of Section 457(f). The dichotomy and uncertainty associated with the varying and fluctuating definitions of substantial risk of forfeiture require the practitioner to exercise extreme care in designing Section 457(f) plans. As more fully explained in Question 20, some Section 457(f) plan designs that have historically been used will violate Section 409A.

Citation: 26 USC Section 409A(d); Treasury Regulation Section 1.409A-1(a)-(b); Preamble to Final 409A Regulations, T.D. 9321, 74 Fed. Reg. 19234 (April 17, 2007) (hereinafter "Final 409A Regulations," or "Final Regulations") § II.B. "Section 457 Plans"; Notice 2007-62, 2007-32 I.R.B. 331, 8-6-2007; PLRs 9030028 and 9041026. For a more detailed discussion of the implications of Notice 2007-62 on 457(f) plans, see Richey, Hopkins & Boekeloo, "Multiple Definitions of Substantial Risk of Forfeiture Create Confusion after § 409A, but Notice 2007-62 Is Not the Answer," 36 Tax Management Compensation Planning Journal 396 (Jan. 2008).

Q.9. Are arrangements involving partnerships subject to Section 409A?

There has been limited IRS guidance on the application of Section 409A to partnerships. Most of the guidance that exists is in the Preamble to the Proposed 409A Regulations, and IRS Notice 2005-1.

Until further guidance is issued, the following rules apply:

- Issuance of a profits interest in connection with performance of services that does not result in inclusion of income by the service provider at the time of issuance is not treated as the deferral of compensation for purposes of Section 409A.
- Issuance of a capital interest in connection with performance of services is treated in the same way for purposes of Section 409A as a grant of equity-based compensation if the compensation is determined by reference to partnership equity.
- The principles applicable to stock options and stock appreciation rights under Section 409A also apply to equivalent rights with respect to partnership interests.
- Section 409A may apply to payments covered by Code Section 707(a)(1) (partner not acting in capacity as partner) if the payments otherwise would constitute deferred compensation under a nonqualified deferred compensation plan.
- Section 409A applies to guaranteed payments described in Section 707(c) and rights to receive such guaranteed payments in the future if the guaranteed payment is for services and the partner providing services does not include the payment in income by the 15th day of the third month following the end of the taxable year of the partner in which the partner obtained a legally binding right to the guaranteed payment, or if later, the taxable year of the partner in which the right to the guaranteed payment becomes no longer subject to a substantial risk of forfeiture.
- An arrangement providing for payments subject to Code Section 736 (payments to a retiring partner or a deceased partner's successor in interest) is generally not subject to Section 409A. The payments must be made pursuant to a written plan on account of retirement and continue at least until the partner's death, the partner cannot render services during the partnership's

taxable year that ends with or within the partner's taxable year of receipt by the partner, there can be no obligations from the other partners to the retired partner, and all of the retired partner's capital must be paid out before the end of the partnership's taxable year. However, payments to a retired partner that do not constitute self-employment income under Code Section 1402(a)(10) are generally subject to Section 409A.

The Treasury and the IRS have requested comments on the application of Section 409A to arrangements involving partnerships and partners, and the ABA Section on Taxation has made a number of suggestions.

Citation: IRS Notice 2005-1, Q&A 7, 1-1-2005; Preamble to Final Regulations; *See also* ABA Tax Section comments at www.abanet.org/tax/pubpolicy/2005/050520eb3.pdf.

Q.10. What constitutes disability pay exempt from Section 409A?

The term "nonqualified deferred compensation plan" does not include a plan, *"or a portion of a plan,"* to the extent that a plan provides bona fide disability pay. Thus, employer-funded or insured plans that provide benefits only in the event of disability are not subject to Section 409A. In addition, payments made under a nonqualified deferred compensation plan in the event of disability constitute disability pay to the extent the disability benefits payable under the plan exceed the present value of the benefits that could be payable to the employee under the nonqualified plan during the employee's lifetime, determined under the plan's optional form of distribution that provides the employee with the largest present value during his or her lifetime.

Example 1. An employer maintains a nonqualified defined benefit plan that provides monthly benefits to an individual commencing at age 65. In the event of a participant's disability before age 65, however, the individual receives $500 per month until age 65, and, upon attaining age 65, will begin receiving the normal monthly benefit provided under the plan in the absence of disability. The portion of the nonqualified plan providing disability benefits constitutes disability pay that is exempt from the requirements of Section 409A. The monthly benefits provided at age 65 constitute deferred compensation that is subject to Section 409A.

Example 2. An employer maintains an account balance plan subject to a vesting schedule. In the event of an individual's disability, however, the individual's account balance becomes fully vested and is distributed in a lump sum. The lump sum payment of benefits upon disability does not constitute disability pay for purposes of the Section 409A regulations because the disability benefit does not exceed the present value of the benefits that could be payable to a participant under the plan during the employee's lifetime (*i.e.*, the employee's account balance). The entire plan is subject to Section 409A.

Citation: Treasury Regulation Section 1.409A-1(a)(5); Treasury Regulation Section 31.3121(b)(2)-1(b)(4)(iv)(C).

Q.11. What are the broad general requirements for nonqualified deferred compensation plans subject to Section 409A?

Section 409A codifies many of the rules previously advanced by the IRS in the area of constructive receipt. In broad terms, Section 409A generally requires that an election to defer compensation must be made before the calendar year in which the compensation is earned; that the form and time of payment of deferred compensation must be established before the compensation is earned; that the time for payment of deferred compensation may generally not be accelerated or further deferred after the compensation is earned, with certain limited exceptions; that deferred compensation may only be paid upon a fixed date, separation from service, or certain other events; and that the deferred compensation arrangement must be documented in writing.

So long as a plan meets these requirements in both form and operation, and so long as the plan remains unfunded (see **Q. 35** and **Q. 44**), the plan will comply with Section 409A and income tax on the amounts deferred will not occur until payment in accordance with plan provisions.

Citation: 26 USC Section 409A(a)(1)(A)(i)(I), which incorporates by reference Sections 409A(a)(2)-(4). The bulk of the Final Regulations merely clarify these major requirements.

DOCUMENTATION REQUIREMENTS

Q.12. Are plans subject to Section 409A required to be in writing?

Yes. (See **Q. 15.**) Therefore, any undocumented arrangement that provides for deferred compensation subject to Section 409A is automatically in violation of Section 409A.

Although it is generally advisable to document any employee benefit plan before it becomes effective, the Section 409A regulations allow documentation to occur as late as the December 31 of the calendar year in which the legally binding right to compensation arises, or, with respect to an amount that is not payable in the calendar year immediately following the calendar year in which the legally binding right arises (the "subsequent year"), by the fifteenth day of the third month of the subsequent year. A plan subject to Section 409A that allows participant elections to defer compensation must set forth in writing the conditions under which such elections may be made no later than the date the initial deferral election becomes irrevocable.

Citation: Treasury Regulation Section 1.409A-1(c)(3).

Q.13. Are there specific features not allowed in plans subject to Section 409A that were commonly included in nonqualified plans prior to enactment of Section 409A?

Except for the distribution events described in the statute and regulations, event-based distributions and all discretionary distributions are prohibited in a deferred compensation plan subject to Section 409A. For example, permitting distribution from a nonqualified plan upon the admission of a participant's child to college was common prior to Section 409A, but is not permitted under the new rules. Similarly, a number of plans formerly provided that a participant could request an early distribution from the plan with the consent of the board of directors of the employer or a committee. Section 409A categorically prohibits such discretionary acceleration of nonqualified plan benefits.

Previously common "haircut" provisions that permitted discretionary distribution at any time if the service provider incurred a penalty, or "haircut," on the amount of the distribution are now prohibited. The authority for such distributions as a substantial limitation on the right to receive immediate payment under Treasury Regulation Section 1.451-2(a) was overridden by Section 409A.

Prior to Section 409A, nonqualified plans commonly permitted the employer to offset any amounts a nonqualified plan participant owed the employer from the amount due the participant under a nonqualified plan. The IRS has informally advised that a salary advance plan that provides an offset against a deferred compensation plan at separation from service violates Section 409A as an impermissible acceleration provision. Therefore, except in the narrow circumstance described in Question 34, such offset provisions are no longer permitted under Section 409A.

Citation: 26 USC Section 409A(a)(2); *See generally* Treasury Regulation Section 1.409A-3 (and the definitions in Treasury Regulation Section 1.409A-1) concerning the limits on distributions and accelerations from plans. See also Congressional Commentary to 26 Section USC 409A, Section 885 of the American Jobs Creation Act of 2004 (Pub. L. No. 108-357) (discussing Section 409A(a)(2) as applied to events-based distributions and "haircut" provisions); IRS CCA Memo 200935029 (8-28-2009) regarding a salary advance plan offset against deferred compensation.

Q.14. Is it appropriate to document the provisions of a plan designed to fall outside the scope of Section 409A?

Plans that are not subject to Section 409A, such as those that satisfy the requirements for the short-term deferral exception (**Q. 17**), are not required to be in writing, but documentation of their provisions demonstrates that they satisfy the requirements for the exception. Documenting a short-term deferral arrangement in writing, in particular, may prove advantageous if for some reason payment is not made within a short-term deferral period and the service recipient does not have a valid excuse for late payment.

Example. An employer maintains an annual bonus plan and specifies in writing that the bonus must be payable by the March 15 following the calendar year in which the bonus is earned. The employer misses the March 15 deadline with no valid excuse, but makes the bonus payment by the end of the year. Because the bonus payment is made after the March 15 deadline but within the same calendar year, the bonus payment will be considered deferred compensation, but will meet the requirements of Section 409A because the arrangement is in writing and the payment is made by the end of the calendar year in which the specified payment date occurs. As stated by Daniel Hogans, one of the architects of the Section 409A regulations, "This is a way to straddle the short-term deferral rule and the required payment deadline." In other words, by documenting the bonus arrangement, payments will be considered exempt from Section 409A if made on or before the March 15 deadline, but will be considered subject to and in compliance with Section 409A if the payments are made after March 15 but before the next December 31. (See **Q. 18.**)

Citation: Annotated version of the Tax Code Section 409A final regulations published in Pension & Benefits Daily (last update November 2008) (hereinafter "Annotated Regulations"), documenting comments of Dan Hogans at BNA's Tax Management audio conference held May 15, 2007, set forth in bold text immediately following Treasury Regulation Section 1.409A-1(b)(4)(ii).

Q.15. What are the minimum documentation requirements for a plan subject to Section 409A?

There is no particular format for documentation of a plan subject to Section 409A, except that it must be documented. A single document is permitted, but two or more documents may also constitute a single plan. Even e-mails or other electronic communications may be sufficient to satisfy the documentation requirements, particularly with respect to participant elections.

At a minimum, the plan must state either the amount of deferred compensation or the method or formula for determining the amount; it must also state the time and form of payment, including initial employee election procedures, and it should contain definitions of key terms that comply with requirements of Section 409A.

Practitioners drafting plans subject to Section 409A should consider inclusion of the following.

For All Plans:

- Definitions with respect to distribution events, such as separation from service, disability, change in control, unforeseeable emergency, and leave of absence. (See **Q. 23-27; Q. 29-32.**)
- A provision for designated payment dates or payment dates measured from the separation date, such as 90 days after separation. (See **Q. 28.**)
- A provision for grandfathering any amounts that were earned and vested on December 31, 2004. (See **Q. 95.**)
- An optional provision for cash-outs of small distributions
- An optional provision for the limited available offset of the service provider's obligations to the service recipient against the amounts due the service provider under the plan. (See **Q. 34.**)
- Optional provisions stating other desired exceptions to the prohibition against benefit accelerations, such as distribution of benefits (i) pursuant to a domestic relations order incident to a divorce or legal separation, (ii) to pay FICA taxes due on compensation deferred under the plan and any associated income taxes, or (iii) to pay taxes due on breach of Section 409A

- If the plan is informally funded through a rabbi trust, a provision prohibiting transfer of assets used to fund the plan to an irrevocable trust in connection with deterioration of the employer's financial health or to an offshore trust
- A provision for voluntary plan termination by the service recipient. (See **Q. 32.**)
- A provision for interpretation of all terms and provisions consistent with Section 409A, especially as to all undefined, ambiguous or incomplete definitions and provisions. (See **Q. 93.**)
- A provision under which the employer either disclaims or accepts responsibility for any adverse tax consequences arising under Section 409A. (See **Q. 38.**)
- A spendthrift or nonassignability provision
- A provision that the plan benefit is an unsecured and unfunded contractual promise to pay plan rather than a funded plan
- Provisions designed to comply with state law employment requirements and choice of law.
- A provision prohibiting setting aside assets in a rabbi trust to informally fund plan benefits during any "restricted period" with respect to a tax-qualified defined benefit pension plan of the employer which does not satisfy certain minimum funding levels. (See **Q. 89.**)

For Any Plan of a Publicly Held Employer:

- A provision for a six-month delay of payments due upon employment termination to a specified employee. (See **Q. 26.**) A plan complies with Section 409A even if it fails to include a six-month delay provision with respect to a service provider who is not a specified employee, provided the six-month delay provision is added no later than the date such a service provider first becomes a specified employee.

For Any Plan That Gives Participants the Right to Select the Time and Form of Payment: (See **Q. 50.**)

- An optional provision allowing for subsequent elections changing the previously designated form and time of payment, including a provision for treating a prior election in installments as a unitary single election or a series of individual elections for this purpose. (See **Q. 54.**).

For an Account Balance Plan:

- A provision for a reasonable rate of return or an objective measure for the rate of return, such as a stock or bond index

For an Elective Deferral Plan:

- A provision stating the date by which elections to defer base pay, bonuses and performance-based pay must be specified, both for existing participants and those who become eligible after the beginning of a year. (See **Q. 51**.)

- If applicable, special provisions for elections to defer performance-based compensation. (See **Q. 51** and **Q. 52**.)

- A provision for treatment of participants whose eligibility terminates and then resumes at a later time. (See **Q. 51**.)

- A provision for automatic cancellation of a participant's deferrals upon the participant's receipt of a hardship distribution. (See **Q. 30** and **Q. 55**.)

For an Employer Non-account Balance Plan:

- A provision prohibiting suspension of payment on reemployment after periodic retirement distributions have begun. (See **Q. 58**.)

Provisions That Are Either Not Permitted or Not Advisable:

- Previously used haircut provisions under which the participant could elect early distribution subject to incurring a penalty, other conditional event-based distributions and accelerations (*e.g.*, if the employee's child goes to college), and certain offset provisions do not satisfy the requirements of Section 409A and must be removed from the plan. (See **Q. 13**.)

- Blanket Section 409A "savings clauses" (*e.g.*, a provision stating "terms which violate Section 409A will be ignored" or "anything needed in this plan is incorporated into this plan") will not cure any Section 409A deficiencies in a plan. A savings clause will not automatically disqualify a plan from meeting the requirements of Section 409A, but it will not bring such a plan into compliance if the plan document includes provisions that contravene or omit requirements under Section 409A or the regulations. However, a provision for application of all terms and provisions consistent with Section 409A, especially as to all undefined, ambiguous or incomplete definitions and provisions, is permissible and useful. The distinction is between reformation of a provision inconsistent with Section 409A and an ambiguous provision that could be interpreted as consistent with Section 409A.

Citation: Treasury Regulation Section 1.409A-1(c)(1)-(3); with respect to Savings Clauses, *see* Annotated Regulations documenting the comments of Stephen Tackney at the ABA Section of Taxation Fall Meeting held September 12, 2008, the comments of William Schmidt at the ALI-ABA Executive Compensation Conference held June 19, 2008, the comments of Stephen Tackney at the ALI-ABA webcast held February 4, 2008, the comments of Stephen Tackney at the POI webcast held on May 9, 2007, and the comments of Dan Hogans at the ALI-ABA conference held June 21, 2007, all of which are set forth in bold text immediately following Treasury Regulation Section 1.409A-1(c)(3)(i); with respect to documenting plan requirements electronically, see Annotated Regulations documenting comments of Dan Hogans at the Steptoe & Johnson LLP audio conference held May 1, 2007, set forth in bold text immediately following Treasury Regulation Section 1.409A-1(c)(3)(iii). Practitioners should also consider in depth the various drafting implications

from Notice 2010-6, 2010-3 I.R.B., 1-19-2010 governing plan documentation error corrections.

SHORT-TERM DEFERRALS

Q.16. Do amounts that are paid shortly after they are earned constitute a deferral of compensation?

Notwithstanding the very broad general definition of the phrase "deferral of compensation" described in Question 3, certain amounts that are paid shortly after they become vested are not considered a deferral of compensation. A deferral of compensation does not occur solely because compensation is paid after the last day of a calendar year as a result of the manner in which the service recipient normally compensates service providers under its payroll system (*e.g.*, an employee renders services to an employer during the last pay period in December but does not receive the paycheck for such services until January pursuant to the employer's standard payroll practices). Additionally, short-term deferrals – amounts that are paid shortly after vesting – are not considered to constitute a deferral of compensation even though compensation payments may be made in a year later than the year in which services relating to the compensation were performed. (See **Q. 17**.)

Citation: Treasury Regulation Section 1.409A-1(b)(3) & (4).

Q.17. What is the short-term deferral rule?

The short-term deferral rule is the most commonly applicable exception to the application of Section 409A. A deferral of compensation does not occur with respect to any payment that is not a "deferred payment," provided that the service provider actually or constructively receives such payment within 2½ months after the close of either the service provider's or service recipient's taxable year in which the payment is no longer subject to a substantial risk of forfeiture (**Q. 16**). Assuming that the service provider's taxable year is the calendar year, then the short-term deferral rule is satisfied if payment is actually or constructively received by the service provider by the March 15 following the close of the calendar year in which the payment is no longer subject to a substantial risk of forfeiture. If the service recipient uses a taxable year other than the calendar year, the deadline for a payment to fall within the short-term deferral rule may be 2½ months after the end of the service recipient's taxable year in which the payment is no longer subject to a substantial risk of forfeiture.

A right to a payment that is never subject to a substantial risk of forfeiture is considered to be no longer subject to a substantial risk of forfeiture on the first day the service provider has a legally binding right to the payment. For example, if an employer first promises on November 15, 2011 to pay an employee a $100,000 bonus, the bonus is considered to no longer be subject to a substantial risk of forfeiture on November 15, 2011. If the bonus is paid by March 15, 2012, it is a short-term deferral.

A "deferred payment" can never constitute a short-term deferral. A payment is a deferred payment if it is made pursuant to a provision of a plan that provides for the payment to be made or completed on or after any date, or upon or after the occurrence of any event, that will *or may* occur later than the end of the applicable 2½ month period. For example, if a service recipient has a legally binding right to compensation that no longer is subject to a substantial risk of forfeiture on November 1, 2011, and the payment is to be made upon the service provider's separation from service, then the payment will not constitute a short-term deferral even if the service provider separates from service shortly after November 1, 2011, and receives payment on or before March 15, 2012. Even though the payment did in fact occur on or before the last day of the applicable 2½ month period, the payment could have occurred at a later date because the service provider could have continued employment beyond March 15, 2012. The arrangement described in this example constitutes a deferral of compensation that is subject to Section 409A.

If a plan provides that the service provider or service recipient may make an election under the plan of a different payment date, schedule or event, such right is disregarded for purposes of the short-term deferral rule. In such cases, whether a plan provides for a deferred payment is determined based on the actual payment date, schedule or event that would apply if no such election were made. If in fact the service provider or service recipient makes an election to defer a payment that would otherwise constitute a short-term deferral, whether the plan provides for a deferred payment is determined based upon the payment date, schedule or event that the service provider or service recipient in fact elected.

The application of the short-term deferral rule to a series of payments depends upon whether payments are designated as a single payment or as separate payments (**Q. 15**). If a series of installment payments is designated as a single payment, then all the installment payments are considered to constitute a deferral of compensation if any one of the payments is or could be made after the applicable 2½ month period. On the other hand, if a stream of payment is designated as separate payments, then those individual payments that are made within the applicable 2½ month period will be considered short-term deferrals if, standing alone, they would satisfy the requirements for short-term deferrals as described above. A common situation in which it may be advantageous to take advantage of the short-term deferral exception for the portion of the stream of payments that may qualify for the exception arises in the separation pay context. To the extent the drafter of a separation pay arrangement designates separation payments as separate payments, some of those payments may constitute short-term deferrals, whereas others may constitute separation pay exempt from Section 409A. (See **Q. 65**.)

As noted above, if a payment actually occurs within the short-term deferral period, it is not subject to Section 409A, and therefore technically need not be documented for purposes of Section 409A. However, if payment actually occurs after the short-term deferral deadline, the payment is subject to Section 409A (including the documentation requirements) unless a special exception applies. (See **Q. 18**.)

A few examples will help illustrate the short-term deferral concept.

Example 1. An employer with a calendar year taxable year awards a bonus to Employee A on November 1, 2010, that is not subject to a substantial risk of forfeiture. The bonus plan does not provide for a payment date or deferred payment. The bonus plan will not be considered to have provided for a deferral of compensation if the bonus is paid or made available to Employee A on or before March 15, 2011. If, however, the bonus payment is not paid or made available to Employee A until a later date, then the bonus arrangement will be subject to Section 409A unless one of the situations justifying delay in payment of compensation specified in Question 18 apply.

Example 2. On November 1, 2008, an employer awards a bonus to an employee subject to forfeiture unless the employee continues working for the employer through December 31, 2010. The employee has the right to make a written election not later than December 31, 2009, to receive the bonus on or after December 31, 2015, but the employee does not make the election. Because the employee does not make a deferral election, the bonus plan will not be considered to have provided for a deferral of compensation if the bonus is paid or made available to the employee on or before March 15, 2011.

Example 3. On November 1, 2008, an employer awards a bonus to an employee under which the employee must continue to perform services through December 31, 2010, to receive the bonus. The bonus plan provides that the bonus is scheduled to be paid in a lump sum on July 1, 2011. Because the plan specifies a payment date after the applicable 2½ month period, the bonus plan provides for a deferral of compensation that does not qualify as a short-term deferral and must comply with Section 409A. This is the case even if the bonus is paid or made available on or before March 15, 2011. Moreover, if the bonus were paid or made available on or before March 15, 2011, this would constitute an impermissible acceleration of a payment in violation of Section 409A, which generally prohibits any acceleration of a payment more than 30 days before the scheduled payment date, in this case, June 1, 2011. (See **Q. 29.**)

Citation: Treasury Regulation Section 1.409A-1(b)(4).

Q.18. What situations justify delay in payment of compensation designed to qualify as a short-term deferral beyond 2½ months after the end of the taxable year in which the compensation is earned?

Compensation designed to satisfy the short-term deferral rule may be paid more than 2½ months after the end of the taxable year in which the compensation is earned and still qualify for the short-term deferral rule in the following three circumstances:

- Administrative impracticability that was not reasonably foreseeable. Payment must occur as soon as administratively practicable.
- The employer is in financial jeopardy as a "going concern." Payment must occur as soon as the financial jeopardy ends.
- The employer would lose its income tax deduction under Code Section 162(m) if the payment were made on time, and, as of the date the legally binding right to the payment arose, the employer reasonably did not anticipate the application of Section 162(m) at the time the payment becomes due. The payment must be made as soon as reasonably practical following the first date on which the service recipient anticipates or reasonably should anticipate that the payment will no longer be restricted by the application of Section 162(m).

It is important to note that this Section 162(m) relief was established for mid-level employees who unexpectedly become subject to Section 162(m) at some later time. According to Daniel Hogans, one of the architects of the regulations, "For someone that you reasonably expect to be subject to Section 162(m), it makes more sense to just have a condition built in that to the extent that the deduction will be limited by 162(m) the amount will be deferred" **(Q. 15)**.

Citation: Treasury Regulation Section 1.409A-1(b)(4)(ii); Annotated Regulations documenting comments of Daniel Hogans at the PriceWaterhouseCoopers webcast held on April 18, 2007, set forth in bold text immediately following Treasury Regulation Section 1.409A-1(b)(4)(ii).

Q.19. What is a substantial risk of forfeiture, and how does it relate to satisfaction of the short-term deferral rule under Section 409A?

Compensation is subject to a substantial risk of forfeiture for purposes of Section 409A if the compensation is conditioned on the performance of substantial future services or the occurrence of a condition related to a purpose of the compensation, and the possibility of forfeiture is substantial. A condition is considered related to the purpose of the compensation only if it relates to the service provider's performance or the service recipient's business activities or organizational goals (for example, the attainment of a prescribed level of earnings of equity value or completion of an initial public offering).

As described in Question 17, the short-term deferral rule exempts compensation from Section 409A if payment occurs within 2½ months after the end of the taxable year in which the service provider obtains a right to the compensation that is not subject to a substantial risk of forfeiture. In some cases, the service provider obtains a vested right to compensation in the year services are rendered. This occurs, for example, with respect to base salary or wages. In such cases, the service provider has no substantial risk of forfeiture once the services are rendered and the requirements of Section 409A apply to any such compensation payment that is deferred beyond the short-term deferral period. In other cases, the compensation may be made subject to a substantial risk of forfeiture, which causes the service provider's vested right to the compensation to be delayed until the substantial risk of forfeiture is satisfied (*e.g.*, a requirement that an employee remain in continuous employment with the employer for a stated period of time or until a stated age in order to obtain a vested right to the deferred compensation). In such cases, the substantial risk of forfeiture and the short-term deferral rule in combination permit a plan that provides for distribution within 2½ months after the end of the year in which the substantial risk of forfeiture expires to avoid application of Section 409A.

Whether the risk of forfeiture is sufficiently substantial depends on the likelihood of its enforcement, based on the facts and circumstances.

One example of compensation subject to a substantial risk of forfeiture is compensation that is payable only if the recipient is continuously employed through the date scheduled for payment of the compensation. To receive payment, the service provider must provide additional services in the form of employment until the date of payment. If payment occurs within the short-term deferral period for the year in which the substantial risk of forfeiture lapses, the payment is exempt from Section 409A under the short-term deferral rule.

Amounts payable only upon involuntary termination are also subject to a substantial risk of forfeiture. For purposes of the short-term deferral rule and the involuntary termination exception, certain types of voluntary "good reason" termination are considered involuntary termination (**Q. 64**).

The regulations address whether compensation is subject to a substantial risk of forfeiture under these other circumstances:

- Voluntary salary deferrals are not subject to a substantial risk of forfeiture.

- A covenant not to compete of itself does not create a substantial risk of forfeiture, even if the compensation is completely forfeitable upon breach of the covenant.

- Compensation is generally not subject to a substantial risk of forfeiture beyond the time at which the recipient otherwise could have elected to receive it, unless the present value of the amount subject to a substantial risk of forfeiture is materially greater than the present value of the amount the recipient otherwise could have elected to receive in the absence of the risk of forfeiture. As a result, subsequent employee deferrals do not satisfy the requirements of Section 409A unless they satisfy the requirements for subsequent elections. (See **Q. 54**.)

- Compensation is generally not subject to a substantial risk of forfeiture following extension of an existing substantial risk of forfeiture to a later date. As a result, rolling vesting dates usually do not create substantial risk of forfeiture. According to William Schmidt, Senior Counsel in the Office of Chief Counsel of the Executive Compensation Branch of the Internal Revenue Service, if compensation is subject to a substantial risk of forfeiture and the forfeiture condition is extended or modified, "as a general rule, unless there is additional consideration paid for that extension, the extension of forfeiture period will be disregarded and the amount will be treated as vested for purposes of 409A."

- Payments contingent on attainment of a prescribed level of earnings may be subject to a substantial risk of forfeiture if the risk of not attaining that level of earnings is substantial.

- Payments contingent on completion of an initial public offering may be subject to a substantial risk of forfeiture if the risk that there will be no public offering is substantial from the outset.

- Stock options that are immediately exercisable in exchange for substantially vested stock are not subject to a substantial risk of forfeiture even if the ability to exercise the option terminates upon separation from service.

For individuals with significant equity voting power in the entity that pays the deferred compensation, the relevant facts and circumstances for determining whether a risk of forfeiture is substantial include:

- The service provider's relationship to other equity holders and the extent of their control, potential control and possible loss of control of the service recipient
- The position of the service provider in the service recipient and the extent to which the service provider is subordinate to other service providers
- The service provider's relationship to the officers and directors of the service recipient
- The person or persons who must approve the service provider's discharge
- Past actions of the service recipient in enforcing the restrictions

Citation: Treasury Regulation Section 1.409A-1(d); Annotated Regulations documenting the comments of William Schmidt at the ABA Section of Taxation fall meeting held on September 12, 2008, reproduced in bold immediately following Treasury Regulation Section 1.409A-1(d)(1).

Q.20. What is the relationship of the definition of substantial risk of forfeiture under Section 409A, Section 83 and Section 457(f)?

The IRS has taken the position that the definition of substantial risk of forfeiture for purposes of section 409A is independent of the definition of the same term for other purposes under the Code. In particular, the definition of substantial risk of forfeiture under Section 83 (which governs the transfer of property in exchange for services) involves a "facts and circumstances" analysis and, as a result, is broader than the Section 409A definition. For example, a provision that requires forfeiture of property upon competition with a prior employer may give rise to a substantial risk of forfeiture for purposes of Section 83, but it does not give rise to a substantial risk of forfeiture for purposes of Section 409A. Similarly, a risk of forfeiture associated with a voluntary deferral of compensation may be treated as substantial under the Section 83 regulations, but will not be recognized as such under the Section 409A regulations unless the present value of the deferred compensation materially exceeds the amount deferred.

Compensation deferred under a nonqualified deferred compensation plan maintained by a tax exempt entity is generally subject to tax in the year in which there is no substantial risk of forfeiture of the right to receive such compensation (a narrow exception exists for compensation deferred under an eligible deferred compensation plan which meets the stringent requirements of Code Section 457(b)). This tax treatment is described in Section 457(f), and ineligible deferred compensation plans maintained by tax exempt and governmental entities are commonly referred to as Section 457(f) plans. The Internal Revenue Service initially applied the Section 83 definition of substantial risk of forfeiture for purposes of Section 457(f) plans. Applying this definition, practitioners frequently designed Section 457(f) plans which included risks of forfeiture which would be considered substantial under Section 83 but not Section 409A. The IRS added an additional level of complexity and confusion by announcing in 2007 that it intends to issue rules that use the Section 409A definition of substantial risk of forfeiture to define a substantial risk of forfeiture for purposes of Section 457(f). No such rules have yet been issued, however.

Tax-exempt and governmental employers which maintain Section 457(f) plans which employ a broad substantial risk of forfeiture definition consistent with Section 83 may potentially run into Section 409A problems, as illustrated by the following examples.

Example 1. A tax-exempt employer has established an arrangement under which a hospital administrator will receive a lump sum payment of $100,000 upon completion of a new wing of the hospital. The $100,000 payment is due to the administrator upon completion of the new wing of the hospital regardless of whether or not the administrator is employed by the hospital at the time the wing is completed, provided that the hospital administrator has not engaged in competition with the hospital prior to completion of the hospital wing. The parties have taken the position that the noncompetition restriction constitutes a substantial risk of forfeiture for purposes of Section 457(f), and it is assumed for purposes of this example that the noncompetition restriction constitutes a substantial risk of forfeiture for purposes of Section 457(f) under all the facts and circumstances. Even though the compensation under this arrangement would result in a deferral of taxation under Section 457(f) under existing rules, the noncompetition restriction does not constitute a substantial risk of forfeiture for Section 409A. Accordingly, the short-term deferral rule does not apply and therefore the arrangement is subject to Section 409A. Moreover, the arrangement violates Section 409A because the compensation is payable upon an impermissible distribution event under Section 409A (*i.e.*, completion of the hospital wing).

Example 2. A tax-exempt employer has established a voluntary deferral arrangement under which an executive has deferred $50,000 of current base pay that the employer has agreed to pay to the employee in a lump sum in five years with interest at the five-year Treasury rate, provided that the employee continues working for the employer during the entire five-year period. Prior to Section 409A, employers took the position under Section 457(f) that this plan design resulted in the deferral of taxation on the compensation until the date of payment because a substantial risk of forfeiture with respect to the right to receive payment continued in effect until the payment date (*i.e.*, the requirement that the employee perform substantial services as a condition to the receipt of the compensation). The Section 409A regulations, however, take the position that a voluntary deferral of compensation will never be subject to a substantial risk of forfeiture unless the present value of the projected payment amount is materially greater than the amount deferred. (See **Q. 19.**) Accordingly, this plan design violates Section 409A.

As a practical matter, a practitioner designing a Section 457(f) plan for a tax-exempt entity must take into account both the Section 409A and 457(f) rules, bearing in mind that the definition of "substantial risk of forfeiture" for purposes of Section 457(f) is in a state of flux and that the definition of substantial risk of forfeiture under Section 83(b) differs from that in Section 409A. Even in the absence of definitive IRS guidance defining substantial risk of forfeiture for purposes of Section 457(f) in the same manner as Section 409A, it is generally prudent to design Section 457(f) plans in a manner such that any substantial risk of forfeiture embedded in such a plan meets the Section 409A definition of substantial risk of forfeiture.

Citation: 26 USC Section 409A(d); Treasury Regulation Section 1.409A-1(a)(b); Preamble to Final 409A Regulations, § II.B. "Section 457 Plans"; Notice 2007-62, 2007-32 I.R.B. 331, 8-6-2007; PLRs 9030028 and 9041026. For a more detailed discussion of the implications of

Notice 2007-62 on 457(f) plans, see Richey, Hopkins & Boekeloo, "Multiple Definitions of Substantial Risk of Forfeiture Create Confusion after § 409A, but Notice 2007-62 Is Not the Answer," 36 Tax Mgmt. Compensation Planning J. 396 (January 2008).

Q.21. What is a vest and pay lump sum SERP?

A vest and pay SERP is a nonqualified employer account balance or nonaccount balance deferred compensation plan that contains a substantial risk of forfeiture and requires distribution in the form of a single sum upon vesting. Benefits accrued under the plan must remain non-vested until the occurrence of a specified event, such as satisfaction of specified age and service requirements, and must be payable in a single sum within 2½ months after the end of the taxable year of vesting. If these requirements are met, the plan will be exempt from Section 409A under the short-term deferral rule. (See **Q. 17.**)

DISTRIBUTION EVENTS

Q.22. What are the primary permissible distribution events under Section 409A?

There are seven primary permissible distribution events. Most are defined more narrowly than under past practice. Event-based distributions are generally prohibited, except as provided in this list. The seven primary permissible distribution events are:

- Separation from service. Different requirements apply to employees versus directors and other independent contractors. (See **Q. 23** and **Q. 24**.) Payment must be delayed for 6 months from the date of separation in the case of specified employees (generally, key employees within the meaning of Code Section 416(i) of a publicly traded company). (See **Q. 26.**)

- Disability. The Social Security definition applies. (See **Q. 27**.)

- Death.

- At a specified time or pursuant to a fixed schedule either stated in the plan or elected on the date of deferral.

- Change in control. This definition is based on the Section 280G golden parachute rules but is narrower. (See **Q. 31**.)

- Unforeseeable emergency. This definition is based on the Section 457 standard but is narrower. (See **Q. 30**.)

- On plan termination. (See **Q. 32**.) If the employer voluntarily terminates a plan, payment must be delayed for 12 months following termination and the employer cannot implement a plan of the same type (**Q. 39**) within three calendar years after the plan termination. Immediate distribution may occur incident to plan termination on the order of a judge in a bankruptcy or reorganization proceeding.

Citation: ***See generally*** **26 USC Section 409A (a)(2); Treasury Regulation Section 1.409A-3.**

Q.23. What is a separation from service that qualifies as a permissible distribution event for an employee under Section 409A?

In General

A distribution to a service provider on separation from service is a permissible distribution event under Section 409A. To satisfy this requirement with respect to a specified employee of a publicly traded company, distribution cannot begin until six months after the separation. (See **Q. 26.**)

In the case of an employee, separation from service includes death, retirement or termination of employment, based on the facts and circumstances in each case.

Termination of Employment of an Employee

The drafters of the regulation were concerned that service providers would attempt to manipulate the timing of distribution by artificially extending or accelerating the date of employment termination. For example, an employee might cease performing all services for an employer but remain on the employer's payroll, and thus claim that no employment termination had occurred such that distribution of his or her nonqualified deferred compensation benefit would be artificially deferred. Or an employee might "terminate" employment but continue to provide services to the employer as an independent contractor, and thereby accelerate the timing of his or her nonqualified plan distribution even though he or she is still working. In order to prevent such manipulation, the Section 409A regulations define termination of employment in terms of the level of services provided by the employee to the employer.

Whether a termination of employment has occurred is determined based on whether the facts and circumstances indicate that the employer and employee reasonably anticipate that no further services would be performed after a certain date or that the level of bona fide services the employee would perform after such date (whether as an employee or as an independent contractor) would permanently decrease to no more than 20% of the average level of bona fide services performed (whether as an employee or an independent contractor) over the immediately preceding 36-month period.

Termination of Employment Presumptions

The regulations set up a series of presumptions in connection with the determination of whether an employee has terminated employment. An employee is presumed to have terminated employment if the level of bona fide services performed decreases to a level equal to 20% or less of the average level of services performed by the employee during the immediately preceding 36-month period.

No presumption regarding termination of employment applies to a decrease in the level of bona fide services performed to a level that is more than 20% and less than 50% of the average level of bona fide services performed during the immediately preceding 36-month period. A termination of employment will be presumed not to have occurred if the service provider continues to provide services at an annual rate that is 50% or more of the services rendered, on average, during the preceding 36 months and the annual remuneration for such services is 50% or more of the average annual remuneration earned during the immediately preceding three full calendar years of employment (or if less, such lesser period).

A plan may treat another level of reasonably anticipated permanent reduction in the level of bona fide services as a termination of employment, provided that the level of reduction required must be designated in writing as a specific percentage, and the reasonably anticipated reduced level of bona fide services must be greater than 20% but less than 50% of the average level of bona fide services provided in the immediately preceding 36 months. Moreover, the plan must specify the definition of separation from service on or before the date on which a separation from service is designated as a time of payment of the applicable amount deferred, and once designated, any change to the definition of separation from service is generally prohibited with respect to amounts previously deferred.

If the plan document does not define what constitutes a separation from service, then the default rule set forth in the regulation will apply.

Example 1. An employee enters into an agreement with his employer under which he will continue on the employer's payroll for two years but only be required to provide services when requested by the employer. In practice, the employee only renders services to the employer one or two days per month. Since the employee is working at a level less than 20% of the average level of services performed during the immediately 36-month period, it is presumed that the employee has terminated employment.

Example 2. An employer and employee enter into an arrangement under which the employee will be paid his or her full compensation for a period of two years, but it is anticipated that the employer will require the employee to render services for only a few hours per week. The parties treat this arrangement as constituting a termination of employment for purposes of Section 409A and, as a result, the employee is paid her entire nonqualified deferred compensation plan account balance pursuant to the terms of such plan. During the first month of this arrangement, the employee works only four hours each week. After a month, however, the employee's replacement unexpectedly terminates employment, and for the next two months the employee works 30 hours per week until another replacement can be found. Even though the employee has worked at a level greater than 50% or more of the average level of services provided during the preceding 36-month period, the presumption that the employee has not terminated employment may be rebutted by the evidence showing that the parties anticipated that the employee's level of services would permanently decrease to no more than 20% of the average level of services over the immediately preceding 36-month period, but unexpected circumstances caused the level of services to increase for a short period of time.

Leaves of Absence

The employment relationship can be treated as continuing uninterrupted during a leave of absence while the service provider is on military leave, sick leave, or other bona fide leave of absence (such as temporary employment by the government) so long as the period of such leave does not exceed six months, or if longer than six months, so long as the individual's right to reemployment with the service recipient is protected by law or contract. In any case, there must be a reasonable expectation that the participant will return to work. If the service provider does not return to work before the expiration of six months or the longer period required by law or contract, the employment relationship is deemed to end on the first date immediately following expiration of the six-month or longer extension period. A special rule applies, however, when the leave of absence is due to any medically determinable physical or mental impairment that can be expected to result in death or to last for a continuous period of not less than six months and such impairment causes the employee to be unable to perform the duties of his or her employment. In this case, a 29-month period of absence may be substituted for the six-month period described above.

The "same-desk rule," formerly used to determine whether an employee has had a separation from service under a tax-qualified 401(k) plan, can be applied by the buyer and seller in a sale of assets to determine whether a separation from service has occurred, so long as it is consistently applied and the intended treatment is specified in writing no later than the closing date. A corporate spin-off or a sale of the stock of a subsidiary does not create a separation from service for purposes of Section 409A if the employee continues to work for the spun off business or the sold subsidiary, respectively.

Citation: 26 USC Section 409A(a)(2)(A)(i); Treasury Regulation Section 1.409A-1(h)(1)(i)-(ii), (h)(4) and (h)(5); Preamble to Final 409A Regulations, Section VII.C.2.f.

Q.24. What constitutes a separation from service of an independent contractor for purposes of Section 409A?

The definition of separation from service of an independent contractor for this purpose is based on the definition of severance from employment in Treasury Regulation Section 1.457-6(b)(2). An independent contractor is generally considered to have severed from employment with the eligible employer upon the expiration of the contract (or in the case of more than one contract, all contracts) under which services are performed for the eligible employer if the expiration constitutes a good faith and complete termination of the contractual relationship. An expiration of a contract does not constitute a good faith and complete termination of the contractual relationship if the eligible employer anticipates a renewal of a contractual relationship or the independent contractor becoming an employee. For this purpose, an eligible employer is considered to anticipate the renewal of the contractual relationship with an independent contractor if it intends to contract again for the services provided under the expired contract, and neither the eligible employer nor the independent contractor has eliminated the independent contractor as a possible provider of services under any such new contract. An eligible employer is considered to intend to contract again for the services provided under an expired contract if the eligible employer's doing so is conditioned only upon having a need for the services, the availability of funds, or both.

A safe harbor exists for a plan that provides for payment of deferred compensation upon a separation from service by an independent contractor. The plan must provide that (i) no deferred compensation amount will be paid to the independent contractor for at least 12 months following the date all relevant contracts expire, and (ii) if the independent contractor begins performing services again for the service recipient prior to the payment of any deferred compensation due upon separation from service, such deferred compensation amount will not be paid until a subsequent separation from service occurs.

Citation: Treasury Regulation Section 1.409A-1(h)(2).

Q.25. When does a separation from service occur when a service provider performs services for a service recipient both as an employee and independent contractor?

If a service provider simultaneously provides services both as an employee and an independent contractor of a service recipient, the service provider must separate from service both as an employee and as an independent contractor to be treated as having separated from service. However, if an employee also serves as a member of a corporate board of directors (or an analogous position for a non-corporate entity), services as a director are not taken into account in determining whether the employee has separated from service as an employee, and vice-versa.

If an individual starts out as an employee and becomes an independent contractor, whether or not a separation from service has occurred will depend upon whether the individual has experienced a separation from service under the employee standard; the rules for determining separation from service under the independent contractor definition will *not* apply.

Example 1. An employer and employee agree that the employee will cease performing services as an employee and become an independent contractor. As an independent contractor, it is anticipated that the employee will provide services of no more than eight hours per month and, in fact, the individual only performs services as an independent contractor for eight hours per month for the next two years. The individual is considered to have separated from service by virtue of the employee separation from service standard.

Example 2. An employee and his employer agree that the employee will cease providing services as an employee and commence providing services to the employer as an independent contractor. The individual continues to receive his full level of pay for his services as an independent contractor, and continues to provide services at a level of 30 hours per week for the next two years. The individual is not considered to have terminated employment merely by virtue of moving to independent contractor status because the level of his services has not permanently ceased to a level below 20% of his prior level of services.

Citation: Treasury Regulation Section 1.409A-1(h)(5); Annotated Regulations documenting comments of William Schmidt at the ABA Section of Taxation meeting on May 9, 2008, set forth in bold text immediately following Treasury Regulation Section 1.409A-1(h)(1)(ii) ("If you start out as an employee and become an independent contractor, the employee standards still apply; you are not going to switch over to the independent contractor definition."); Annotated Regulations documenting the comments of Stephen Tackney at the Section 409A Compliance & Drafting Challenges ALI-ABA webcast held February 4, 2008, set forth in bold text immediately following Treasury Regulation Section 1.409A-1(h)(5)

("Regarding the limited application of the rule to the employee/independent contractor status, the regulations are talking about moving from employee to independent contractor, about the general proposition that you have not separated from service merely because you have changed status. Look at the specific rules about being an employee.").

Q.26. Must 409A plans for some employers require delayed payments to some plan participants (called "specified employees"), even though there is a permissible separation from service?

Yes. Publicly traded companies must delay the distribution of Section 409A plan benefits to defined specified employees for six full calendar months. A publicly traded company is one whose shares are publicly traded on an established securities market or otherwise. This includes a subsidiary whose parent company is publicly traded or an affiliate of a company that is publicly traded. For this purpose, an established securities market includes:

- A national securities exchange registered under the Securities Exchange Act of 1934 (*e.g.*, the New York Stock Exchange)
- Foreign national securities exchanges that are officially recognized by a governmental authority (*e.g.*, Tokyo stock exchange)
- Over-the-counter markets such as Nasdaq

The six-month delay rule applies to separation from service situations only, including small cash-out distributions. (See **Q. 29.**) The six-month delay rule does *not* apply to the following situations:

1. Benefits paid due to:

- Death
- Disability
- Change in ownership or effective control
- Unforeseen emergency

2. Accelerations of distributions due to:

- Domestic relations orders
- Satisfying a federal, state or local conflict of interest law
- Payment of employment taxes

Definition of Specified Employee: A specified employee is defined by reference to the term "key employee" under the top-heavy qualified plan rules (Section 416(i)). A person constitutes a specified employee if he or she falls within one of the following categories at any time during the 12-month period ending on the "specified employee identification date" (the default is December 31):

- A 5% owner of employer;
- A 1% owner with compensation greater than $150,000 (not indexed); or
- A corporate officer with compensation greater than $160,000 (indexed annually, as of 2010)

Note: As to officers making more than $160,000 (in 2010):

- This group is generally limited to 10% of all employees.
- For companies with fewer than 30 employees, the number of officers included is the lesser of three or the actual number of officers.
- For companies with more than 500 employees, the maximum number of officers is 50.

Default Rules for Identifying Specified Employees. Unless the service recipient elects otherwise, the determination of who constitutes a specified employee is made as follows:

- Those individuals who would be considered key employees under Section 416(i) at any time during the 12-month period ending on December 31 (the "specified employee identification date") are identified;
- The individuals identified in Step One above are considered specified employees for the 12-month period commencing on the next following April 1 (the "specified employee effective date");
- For purposes of identifying key employees in Step One above, the definition of compensation set forth in Treasury Regulation Section 1.415(c)-2(a) is applied.

Alternative Approaches for Identifying Specified Employees. In lieu of the definition above, a service recipient may make the following elections with respect to determining who constitutes a specified employee:

- A service recipient may designate any date other than December 31 as the specified employee identification date, provided that the same specified employee identification date must be used with respect to all nonqualified deferred compensation plans of the service recipient, and any change to the specified employee identification date may not be effective for a period of at least 12 months.
- A service recipient may designate any date following the specified employee identification date as the specified employee effective date, provided that such date may not be later than the first day of the fourth month following the specified employee identification date, and provided further that a service recipient must use the same specified employee effective date

with respect to all nonqualified deferred compensation plans, and any change to the specified employee effective date may not be effective for a period of at least 12 months.

- The service recipient may elect to use any available definition of compensation under the Section 415 regulations, provided that the definition is applied consistently to all employees of the service recipient for purposes of identifying specified employees. Once a list of specified employees has become effective, the service recipient cannot change the definition of compensation for purposes of identifying specified employees for the period during which such list is effective.

- The service recipient may elect to expand the number of individuals who will be considered specified employees using an objectively determinable standard which provides no direct or indirect election to any service provider regarding its application, provided the method used results in either all service providers or no more than 200 service providers being identified as specified employees as of any date.

- A service recipient may elect to not take into account certain compensation excludable from a nonresident alien's gross income. This rule generally allows a service recipient to not count a nonresident alien working outside the United States as among the highest 50 paid officers.

Any of the elections described above are effective only after all necessary corporate action has been taken to make such elections binding for purposes of all affected nonqualified deferred compensation plans in which the affected service providers participate. If a service recipient attempts to make one of the elections described above but such election is not binding on all affected nonqualified deferred compensation plans and applied consistently to all affected service providers, the election is void and the default rules apply. Accordingly, a service recipient desiring to make one of these elections will want to do so in a manner where it is clear that the election applies to all affected nonqualified plans and service providers. This may be done effectively through a board resolution. Note that merely including an election in one nonqualified plan document of the employer may prove ineffective if the same election provisions are not included in other nonqualified plans maintained by the employer.

Summary of steps for determining specified employees.

1. Identify the specified employee "identification date" in the plan document. If not specified, the default date will be December 31 of the prior plan year. In general, this is the only date on which specified employees will be identified. This date can be changed in the future, but any modification cannot be effective until 12 months after the date the decision to change the identification date has been made.

2. Using the identification date, determine the "effective date." The effective date is the date for the employees identified under Step 1 to be treated as specified employees for the delay rule. That date is the first day of the fourth month following the identification date under the default rule. For example, if the specified employee identification date is *December 31*, then the specified employee effective date is April 1, and the employee will be a specified employee until the following March 31. The list of employees as of the effective date will be those subject to the delay rule for a period of 12 months until the new list is determined.

3. Determine whether the employee is a specified employee on the date of a separation from service. If an individual is on the list of specified employees during the 12-month period determined in Step 2, then the delay rule must be applied to a distribution.

For all publicly traded companies, the sponsor should provide a list of "specified employees" for the coming plan year from which the administrator can work to determine if a delay of distribution must occur in case of separation from service. To the extent a public company wishes to avoid the exercise of determining the list of specified employees each year, the plan may be designed to provide a six-month delay of payment upon separation from service for all participants, not just specified employees.

Design Considerations. If a plan distribution to a specified employee must be delayed for six months, plan terms can allow either (i) a delayed start of all payments, or (ii) a lump-sum distribution of any delayed payments six months following separation from service followed by continuance of the balance of any payments due. Interest may be added to any delayed payments.

Corporate Transactions Involving Two Public Companies. Special default specified employee identification rules apply in the context of corporate mergers and acquisitions. Generally, when one publicly traded corporation acquires another publicly traded corporation, the combined organization uses the next specified employee identification date and next specified employee effective date of the acquiring corporation. In addition, the combined organization may combine the lists of specified employees at each organization as of the date of acquisition and treat the top 50 most highly compensated officers (along with certain owners) as specified employees between the date of the acquisition and the next specified employee effective date.

The default merger and acquisition rules do not affirmatively address the identification of specified employees of the combined corporation after the first specified employee effective date but before the next specified employee identification date following the acquisition. As noted earlier, the final regulations merely note that the acquiring corporation's specified employee next effective date and identification dates are used after the acquisition. However, the final regulations do not appear to consider the specified employee identification procedure to be used if the next specified employee effective date occurring after the acquisition occurs before the next specified employee identification date occurring after the acquisition. IRS officials have not clarified the default rules that apply in this situation in their informal discussions of the final Section 409A regulations.

In this situation, the most reasonable reading of the default rules is that the specified employee identification date is the acquiring corporation's specified employee most recent identification date that occurred prior to the acquisition. However, it is unclear whether only officers of the acquiring corporation or officers of both the acquiring and acquired corporation are tested for key employee status as of such specified employee identification date. On the one hand, it seems reasonable to conclude that if the specified employee identification date is taken from the acquiring corporation, only the officers of such acquiring corporation as it actually existed prior to the acquisition should be considered. On the other hand, it also seems reasonable to conclude that because the officers of the acquired corporation are clearly considered in determining specified employee status after the acquisition and before the first specified employee effective date after the acquisition, such officers would also be considered after such first effective date. Either construction is supportable under the default specified employee identification rules.

Example: Assume one public company acquires another public company on January 10, 2011, and that the acquiring company uses the default rules for determining specified employees (December 31 specified employee identification date and April 1 specified employee effective date). It is clear under the default rules that the post-acquisition key employee identification and effective dates will be December 31 and April 1, respectively. It is also clear that between January 10, 2011 and March 31, 2011, the default rules require combining the lists of specified employees of both the acquirer and target as of January 10, 2011, and deeming the top 50 most highly compensated officers as the "specified employees" of the combined entity (along with certain owners) until March 31, 2011. A practitioner could reasonably construe the default specified employee identification rules such that no officer of the target is a specified employee commencing April 1, 2011, based on the fact that no such officer worked for a member of the acquirer's controlled group as of December 31, 2010. A practitioner could also apply the specified employee identification procedures by assuming that officers of the target were officers of and earned their compensation from the acquirer at all times prior to the acquisition.

Corporate Transactions Involving a Public and Nonpublic Service Recipient. If a public and nonpublic service recipient combine through a corporate transaction and the resulting company is a public company, the resulting public company's next specified employee identification date and specified employee effective date following the corporate transaction are the specified employee identification date and specified employee effective date that the initial public company would have been required to use absent such transaction. For the period after the date of the corporate transaction and before the next specified employee effective date, the specified employees of the initial public company before the transaction continue to be the specified employees of the resulting public company following the transaction, and no service providers of the initial private company are required to be treated as specified employees.

Spinoffs. If as part of a corporate transaction a public company becomes two or more separate public companies, the next specified employee identification date of each of the post-transaction public companies is the specified employee identification date that the public company before the transaction would have been required to use absent such transaction. For the period after the date of the corporate transaction and before the next specified employee effective date, the specified employees of the public company immediately before the transaction continue to be the specified employees of the post-transaction public companies.

Alternative Rules for Corporate Transactions. Notwithstanding the default rules, the final Section 409A regulations permit an acquiring corporation to utilize any reasonable method for identifying specified employees after a corporate transaction, provided that all corporate action necessary to effectuate this reasonable method under all nonqualified deferred compensation plans is taken within 90 days of the transaction and the method is applied consistently after adopted.

Citation: *See generally* Treasury Regulation Section 1.409A-1(i).

Q.27. What is the definition of disability for purposes of Section 409A?

Disability is a permissible distribution event under Section 409A. To satisfy the requirements for distribution on account of disability, the service provider must either be:

- Unable to engage in any substantial gainful activity by reason of a medically determinable physical or mental impairment that can be expected to result in death or can be expected to last for a continuous period of not less than 12 months, or

- Receiving income replacement benefits for a period of not less than three months under an accident and health plan covering employees of the employer by reason of any medically determinable physical or mental impairment that can be expected to last for a continuous period of not less than 12 months.

This is the definition of disability used under Social Security. Treatment of the inability to engage in the individual's own occupation does not satisfy this standard.

Citation: 26 USC Section 409A(a)(2)(C)); Treasury Regulation Section 1.409A-3(i)(4)(i)-(iii).

Q.28. Once a distribution event occurs entitling a plan participant to receive payment, when must the payment be made?

A plan that provides payment upon a permissible distribution event must provide that payment is made on the date of such event or upon another payment date that is objectively determinable and nondiscretionary at the time the event occurs. For example, a plan might provide that nonqualified deferred compensation is paid upon separation from service, or the plan might provide that nonqualified deferred compensation is paid on the 30th day after separation from service. The regulations require that payment be made:

- On the payment date specified; or

- Upon any later date within the same calendar year; or

- By the fifteenth day of the third calendar month following the specified payment date, provided that the service provider is not permitted to designate the taxable year of the payment; or

- No earlier than 30 days before the designated payment date, provided the service provider is not permitted to designate the taxable year of the payment.

Example 1. A plan provides that payment of deferred compensation will be made upon separation from service. A participant separates from service on June 1, 2010. Payment may be made as early as May 1, 2010, and as late as December 31, 2010. If instead the individual had separated from service on December 1, 2010, payment could be made as early as November 1, 2010, and as late as February 15, 2011, provided that the participant is not allowed to elect the taxable year of the payment.

Example 2. A plan provides that payment of deferred compensation will be made in a lump sum when a participant has both separated from service and signed a release of all claims against the employer. Because the employee may manipulate the time when the deferred compensation will be paid by choosing the date he or she will execute the release, the payment date is not objectively determinable and nondiscretionary at the time the separation from service occurs. Accordingly, the nonqualified plan violates Section 409A. One way the arrangement could be modified to comply with Section 409A is to provide that the deferred compensation will be paid 90 days after separation from service if, and only if, the participant has executed a release of claims on or before such date.

Citation: Treasury Regulation Section 1.409A-3(c) & (d); Notice 2010-6, 2010-3 I.R.B., 1-6-2010); for a comprehensive analysis of the interplay between Section 409A and releases, see Oringer, Release Us From Confusion Over Nonqualified Deferred Compensation, 36 Tax Mgmt. Compensation Planning J. 223 (Oct. 2008).

ACCELERATION OF BENEFITS

Q.29. May deferred compensation distributions be accelerated?

Generally no. Acceleration is permitted only in limited circumstances, as follows:

- *By Statute*:
  - Unforeseeable emergency (**Q. 30**)
  - Change in control (**Q. 31**)
  - Disability (**Q. 27**)
  - Death
- *By Regulation*:
  - Plan termination (**Q. 32**)
  - Domestic relations order (**Q. 2**)
  - Compliance with conflict of interest laws (**Q. 2**)
  - To fund employment and state, federal and foreign withholding taxes, including those due on vesting under a Section 457(f) plan
  - To fund taxes due on account of income inclusion upon failure to comply with Section 409A
  - Cash-outs (limited to the Code Section 402(g)(1)(b) elective deferral maximum for the year of distribution, $16,500 in 2010)

- To avoid imposition of the excise taxes imposed under Code Section 409(p). This tax may be imposed if synthetic equity (which includes deferred compensation) and employer stock held under an employee stock ownership plan sponsored by an S corporation become overly concentrated in certain individuals who, with their family members, own a majority of the S corporation.

Citation: 26 USC Section 409A(a)(2)(A)(i)-(vi); Treasury Regulation Section 1.409A-3(i)(4)(ii)-(vii) and (ix)-(xi).

Q.30. What is an unforeseeable emergency for purposes of Section 409A?

For purposes of Section 409A, an unforeseeable emergency is a severe financial hardship of the service provider resulting from an illness or accident of the service provider or the service provider's spouse or dependent within the meaning of Code Section 152(a); loss of the service provider's property due to a casualty loss; or any other extraordinary and unforeseeable circumstances arising as a result of events beyond the control of the service provider. A distribution on account of a qualifying unforeseeable emergency cannot exceed the amount necessary to satisfy the emergency plus the taxes reasonably anticipated as a result of the distribution. The distribution must also take into account the extent to which the hardship need is or may be relieved by reimbursement or compensation from insurance or otherwise, or by the liquidation of the participant's assets, except to the extent that such liquidation itself would cause a severe financial hardship. A plan's administrative procedures should include a process sufficient to demonstrate operational compliance with Section 409A and no intent to circumvent the requirements of Section 409A by use of plan provisions for distribution on unforeseeable emergency.

Citation: 26 USC Section 409A(a)(2)(B)(ii); Treasury Regulation Section 1.409A-1(i)(3)(i)-(iii).

Q.31. What is a change in ownership or effective control for purposes of Section 409A?

A plan may permit plan termination and distribution of all benefits upon the occurrence of a change in ownership or effective control of a corporation, or a change in ownership of a substantial portion of the corporation's assets. The definition of change in ownership or effective control for this purpose is unique to Section 409A.

In general, a change in control or effective ownership requires a 50% or more change in ownership of a corporation; a change in effective control requires a 30% or more acquisition of voting power or a hostile election of a majority of directors over a 12-month period. A change in ownership of a substantial portion of assets requires acquisition of 40% or more of a corporation's assets during a 12-month period. Acquisition of an equity position by the federal government or another entity pursuant to the Emergency Economic Stabilization Act of 2008 on or after June 4, 2009, will not be considered a change in ownership or effective control that would permit a distribution of deferred compensation pursuant to Section 409A.

Citation: 26 USC Section 409A(a)(2)(A)(V); Treasury Regulation 1.409A-1(i)(5)(i)-(vii); Notice 2005-1, 2005 C.B. 274 (12-20-2004) Q&As 11-14; Notice 2009-49, 2009-25 I.R.B. 1093 (6-4-2009).

Q.32. In what circumstances may an employer terminate or liquidate a plan that is subject to Section 409A?

Prior to the effective date of Section 409A, employers could terminate and liquidate plans without limitation other than those contained in the plan. The regulations permit termination in only three situations:

- Employer voluntary termination, subject to the following:
  - All plans of the same 409A type **(Q. 39)** must also be terminated with respect to all participants (*e.g.*, all elective deferral account balance plans, all employer account balance plans).
  - A new plan of the same type may not be established for at least three years.
  - No payments other than those otherwise payable under the terms of the plan can be made during the 12 months following the date of plan termination.
  - All payments must be made within 24 months following the date of plan termination.
- Termination in connection with a change in control of the employer. All plans of the same Section 409A type (**Q. 39**) that are maintained by the service recipient immediately after the change in control must be terminated with respect to each participant that experienced the change in control. Benefits must be paid during the period beginning 30 days before and ending 12 months after the change in control. (See **Q. 31.**)
- Termination in connection with corporate dissolution taxed under Code Section 331 or with the approval of a bankruptcy court. The amounts deferred under the plan must be included in the participants' gross income by the end of the calendar year in which the plan termination occurs, the end of the calendar year in which the deferred amount is no longer subject to a substantial risk of forfeiture, or the end of the first calendar year in which the payment is administratively practicable, whichever is last.

Citation: Treasury Regulation Section 1.409A-3(j)(4)(ix).

Q.33. Does acceleration of vesting of deferred compensation in and of itself cause a problem under Section 409A?

No, as long as the acceleration of vesting does not result in an acceleration of the time for payment of deferred compensation. However, acceleration of vesting could constitute a material modification of a grandfathered plan in existence on or before October 3, 2004, and could cause such a plan to lose its grandfathered status. (See **Q. 96.**)

Citation: ***See generally*** **Treasury Regulation Section 1.409A-3(a); Notice 2005-1, 2005-1 C.B. 274 (12-20-2004) Q&A 15.**

Q.34. Does Section 409A prohibit forfeiture, reduction or voluntary relinquishment of deferred compensation?

No. Forfeiture or voluntary relinquishment of deferred compensation of itself is not treated as a distribution of the amount forfeited or relinquished under Section 409A. However, if the service provider receives or acquires the right to receive a different form of compensation in connection with the forfeiture or relinquishment, the series of transactions may be treated as a distribution under Section 409A. For example, if a service provider forfeits a right to receive deferred compensation due in a future year and simultaneously receives the right to current compensation roughly equal to the value of the amount forfeited, the IRS would view the combination of these two events as an impermissible acceleration of payment of the deferred compensation in violation of Section 409A. Likewise, if a deferred compensation plan contains a provision that any amount due the service provider under the plan will be offset by amounts the service provider owes the service recipient, such as a salary advance, an impermissible acceleration will generally occur if the employer effects such an offset. This type of offset provision is permitted only if the service provider's debt was incurred in the ordinary course of the service relationship, the amount offset does not exceed $5,000 in any taxable year, and the offset is taken at the same time and in the same amount as payment of the debt would otherwise have been due.

It was previously common for plans to include generic offset provisions. Such provisions are not allowed under Section 409A, but can be eliminated or revised in 2010 to comply with the requirements of Section 409A prior to the occurrence of an offset without penalty under Notice 2010-6.

Citation: ***See generally*** **26 USC Section 409A(a)(3);** ***see also*** **Treasury Regulation Section 1.409A-3(f), Treasury Regulation Section 1.409A-3(j)(4); CCA 200935029, 8-28-2009; Notice 2010-6, 2010-3 I.R.B. 275 (1-5-2010).**

Citation: Treasury Regulation Section 1.409A-1(b)(4)(ii).

TAX CONSEQUENCES

Q.35. What is the general federal income tax scheme for plans subject to Section 409A?

In the absence of a breach of the requirements of Section 409A, federal income tax is imposed on nonqualified deferred compensation in the year in which payment is actually or constructively received. Payments are taxable as ordinary income at then current rates.

There are three negative tax consequences in the event of a breach of the requirements of Section 409A:

- The entire amount of the participant's vested account balance in the case of an individual account plan (see **Q. 47**) or the present value of the participant's vested benefit in the case of a nonaccount balance plan (see **Q. 49**) as of the end of the tax year in which the breach occurs under all plans of the same type (see **Q. 39**) is treated as ordinary income for the year of breach, whether or not distributed in that year. It is possible that nonvested benefits would also be treated as ordinary income for the year if, based on the facts and circumstances, there is an attempt to evade Section 409A.

- An additional excise tax is imposed on the participant equal to 20% of the amount treated as ordinary income.

- The income tax imposed is increased by a premium interest tax equal to the amount of interest at the underpayment rate (established under Code Section 6621) plus one percentage point on the underpayments that would have occurred had the deferred compensation been includible in income for the taxable year in which first deferred or, if later, the first taxable year in which such deferred compensation is not subject to a substantial risk of forfeiture. This requires the service provider to allocate the amount required to be taken into income to the respective calendar years in which it was first deferred or became vested, if later; recalculate the income tax for each such year including the additional deferred compensation as income; determine the hypothetical underpayment of taxes that would have resulted had such deferred amounts been includible in income when first deferred or vested; and then determine the interest that would have been due upon the hypothetical underpayment based upon the premium interest rate (*i.e.*, the underpayment rate plus one percentage point). In practice, it may be almost as costly to pay someone to compute the premium interest tax as the amount of the premium interest tax itself.

IRS proposed regulations generally would apply the adverse tax consequences that result from a failure to comply with Section 409A with respect to amounts deferred under a plan in the year in which noncompliance with Section 409A occurs and all previous taxable years, but only to the extent such amounts are not subject to a substantial risk of forfeiture and have not previously been included in income. Accordingly, a failure to meet the requirements of Section 409A during a calendar year generally would not affect the taxation of amounts deferred under the plan for a subsequent year during which the plan complies with Section 409A in form and operation.

Under this general rule, if all of a service provider's deferred amounts under a plan are nonvested on the last day of the year in which a Section 409A violation occurs, the nonvested deferred amounts generally would not be includible in income under Section 409A in the year of the violation. If the violation were corrected before the year in which the service provider becomes vested in the deferred amount, no adverse tax consequences would arise under Section 409A. In other words, to the extent that Section 409A violations are corrected before the calendar year in which any amounts under a plan become vested, no adverse Section 409A tax consequences ensue. To ensure that this rule does not become a means for taxpayers to disregard the requirements of Section 409A, however, the proposed Section 409A regulations would disregard a substantial risk of forfeiture for purposes of determining the amount includible in income under

Section 409A with respect to nonvested deferred amounts if the facts and circumstances indicate that the service recipient has a pattern or practice of permitting impermissible changes in the time and form of payment with respect to nonvested deferred amounts.

California imposes its own additional 20% state excise tax in the event of a breach of Section 409A. (See **Q. 45.**)

Citation: *See generally* 26 USC Section 409A(a)(1)(A)(i)(II) and (B); Proposed Treasury Regulation Section 1.409A-4.

Q.36. Who is responsible for payment of the taxes imposed on account of a breach of Section 409A?

Even though the service recipient is generally responsible for documentation and operation of the plan, the service provider is responsible for payment of these taxes, and the service recipient does not lose its expense deduction incident to the taxable deemed distribution arising from a Section 409A violation.

The adverse tax consequences associated with noncompliance could be shifted from the service provider to the service recipient by an indemnity or other contractual provision in the plan document. (See **Q. 38.**)

Citation: 26 USC Section 409A(a)(1)(A)(ii); *See generally* Proposed Treasury Regulation Section 1.409A-4.

Q.37. What constitutes a violation of Section 409A that causes a service provider to incur tax liability under Section 409A?

Section 409A requires compliance in both form and operation with its required restrictions on elections, distributions, and accelerations. Any violation must be corrected in accordance with the guidance provided in IRS Notices 2008-113 for operational errors or Notice 2010-6 for documentation errors, or the additional taxes imposed in connection with violation of Section 409A will apply with respect to vested amounts. (See **Q. 35.**)

Citation: IRC 409A(a)(1)(A); Prop. Treasury Regulation 1.409A-4; Notice 2008-113, 2008-51 I.R.B. 1305 (12-5-2008); IRS Notice 2010-6, 2010-3 I.R.B. 275 (1-5-2010).

Q.38. Is an employer required to indemnify plan participants against the taxes imposed by Section 409A if the related violation of Section 409A is due to the employer's own action or inaction?

No. The plan document may include express acceptance or disclaimer of responsibility not only for the taxes due, but also for the service provider's costs of audit and litigation, depending on the intention of the parties. (See **Q. 15.**)

Citation: Treasury Regulation Section 1.409A-3(i)(1)(v).

Q.39. What is the aggregation rule, and how does it apply to determine federal income tax liability on account of a violation of Section 409A?

In the event of an operational violation of Section 409A, a service provider's vested amounts under all plans of the same type as the plan under which the breach occurred are aggregated for purposes of determining the federal income tax consequences of the breach, including the amount subject to ordinary income tax for the year of the breach and the amount of the additional taxes imposed by Section 409A. If the service provider participates in several plans of the same type, they are all aggregated for this purpose, but if the service provider participates in two or more different types of plans, then the plans are not aggregated for this purpose.

There are nine plan types for this purpose:

- Participant elective deferral account balance plans (examples: voluntary elective salary and bonus deferral plans)
- Employer account balance plans (examples: employer matching contributions under a defined contribution plan, phantom stock plans, and cash balance plans, even though they are treated as defined benefit plans under the tax-qualified plan rules)
- Employer nonaccount balance plans (example: defined benefit supplemental executive retirement plans other than cash balance plans)
- Stock equity plans (examples: stock appreciation rights, nonqualified stock option plans)
- Severance/separation pay plans payable solely on an involuntary separation from service or as a result of participation in a window program
- Split-dollar life insurance plans
- Foreign plans
- Reimbursements/fringe benefit plans
- Other miscellaneous types of plan

Plans for employees are not aggregated with plans of the same type for outside directors of the employer or other independent contractors. Plans of the same type for independent directors and other independent contractors are aggregated with each other.

The plan aggregation rules described above do not apply to the requirement that a plan be documented in writing. Accordingly, deferrals of compensation under an arrangement that fails to meet the Section 409A requirements solely due to a failure to meet the written plan requirements are not aggregated with deferrals of compensation under other plans that meet such requirements.

The aggregation rules also apply in the context of other aspects of Section 409A, including elections to defer (see **Q. 51)** and distributions on plan termination. (See **Q. 32.**)

Citation: Treasury Regulation Section 1.409A-1(c)(2) and Section 1.409A-1(c)(3)(viii); Annotated Regulations documenting the comments of Daniel Hogans at the Steptoe & Johnson LLP audio conference held on May 1, 2007, reproduced in bold immediately following Treasury Regulation Section 1.409A-1(c)(2)(i)(C)(2) ("Cash balance plans are account balance plans consistent with 3121(v)").

Q.40. What is a documentary violation of Section 409A?

A documentary violation occurs when the plan document does not comply with the requirements of Section 409A, for example, if it contains a "haircut" provision that permits the service provider to accelerate distribution with a penalty (**Q. 13**).

Q.41. What is the effect of a documentary violation of Section 409A?

All vested deferred compensation of all service providers accrued under the plan as of the effective date of the noncomplying provision and thereafter is subject to the taxes imposed by Section 409A, but all plans of the same type are *not* aggregated for this purpose. (See **Q. 39**.)

Q.42. What is an operational violation of Section 409A?

An operational violation occurs when the plan provisions comply with Section 409A, but the plan is administered otherwise, for example, if the plan provides for distribution to a service provider in one taxable year and by inadvertence, the distribution occurs in an earlier or later taxable year.

Q.43. What is the effect of an operational violation of Section 409A?

An operational violation of Section 409A causes adverse tax consequences only with respect to the individuals affected by the violation, not the entire plan, but it will affect the federal income tax treatment of all vested interests of that individual under all plans of the same type. (See **Q. 39**.) The existence of nine plan types and the disaggregation of plans for employees and plans for independent contractors limit the amounts at risk in connection with a particular violation of Section 409A. For example, if an employer maintains an employer nonaccount balance plan for an employee and establishes another employer nonaccount balance plan for the same employee, the employee's interests under both plans are taken into account in determining the employee's federal income tax liability if either plan violates Section 409A. If the employer establishes an employer account balance plan for the same employee instead of a nonaccount balance plan, then if one plan violates Section 409A but the other does not, only the employee's interest under the plan that violates Section 409A is taken into account in determining the employee's federal income tax liability in connection with the violation.

Citation: ***See generally*** **26 USC Section 409A(a)(1)(A)(ii); Treasury Regulation Section 1.409A-1(c)(2) as to aggregation rule generally and categories; Treasury Regulation Section 1.409A-2(a)(7) as to elections; Treasury Regulation Section 1.409A-3(i)(4)(ix) as to plan terminations & liquidations.**

Q.44. Does Section 409A replace all prior law governing federal income taxation of unfunded deferred compensation arrangements?

No. The requirements and doctrines of prior federal income tax law, such as the economic benefit, constructive receipt and nonassignability rules, remain applicable to plans subject to Section 409A except to the extent that Section 409A changed the prior law. The legislative history is clear that Section 409A is only intended to clarify the constructive receipt doctrine. Therefore, plans must comply both with Section 409A and the prior tax law, except to the extent Section 409A has specifically replaced that prior tax law. The prior income tax law therefore also continues to govern plans that may be exempt or excepted from Section 409A coverage, such as grandfathered plans, plans that satisfy the short-term deferral rule, and plans of tax-exempt entities governed by Section 457(b) (**Q. 2**). The same is true for making corrections of operational or documentary errors on plans exempt or excepted from Section 409A. (See **Q. 93** and **Q. 94**.)

Citation: 26 USC Section 409A(c); H.R. Rep. No. 108-548 (Ways and Means Committee report on H.R. 4520), 276 (June 16, 2004), Doc 2004-12632, 2004 TNT 118-7.

Q.45. Have any states imposed a personal income tax that parallels Section 409A?

Yes. One state, California, has enacted a 20% state excise tax applicable to amounts subject to a violation of Section 409A. When one considers the combination of federal and state ordinary income tax, the federal and state 20% excise taxes, the federal Social Security and Medicare taxes and the interest penalty under Section 409A, a violation of Section 409A in California is devastating.

Citation: California takes the position that Cal. Rev. Tax Code Section 17501 automatically incorporates into California tax law the provisions of Section 409A. See California Franchise Tax Board Statement in Tax News, May 2008 Edition as to California adoption of 409A correction procedures, and current Form 540 Instructions, Line 33.

Q.46. Can the negative income tax consequences of a breach of Section 409A be mediated?

Yes, on prompt identification and correction of a breach in either form or operation under Notice 2008-113 (for operational errors) and/or Notice 2010-6 (for form errors). (See **Q. 93** and **Q. 94**.) California has adopted parallel correction procedures. Also, California does not require the notice reporting required by the IRS in cases of a violation of Section 409A. (See **Q. 45**.)

PLANS SUBJECT TO SECTION 409A THAT HAVE HISTORICALLY BEEN CONSIDERED DEFERRED COMPENSATION PLANS

Q.47. How are participant account balance plans treated under Section 409A?

Participant account balance plans are a separate plan type for purposes of Section 409A. (See **Q. 39.**) These plans require voluntary employee or independent contractor elections to defer compensation earned and otherwise payable in the current year, such as salary, fees, bonus or commissions, so the amounts deferred and any appreciation and earnings thereon are typically 100% vested at all times (*i.e.*, are not made subject to a substantial risk of forfeiture). (See **Q. 19.**) However, if the plan complies with Section 409A and other law governing constructive receipt, in both form and operation, federal income tax will be deferred until distribution as provided for under the plan.

Citation: ***See generally*** **26 USC Section 409A(a); Treasury Regulation Section 1.409A-1 – 3.**

Q.48. How are employer account balance plans treated under Section 409A?

Employer account balance plans are a separate plan type for purposes of Section 409A. (See **Q. 39.**) Typical employer account balance plans are based on the employer's promise to make future payments to supplement the employer's contributions under a tax-qualified defined contribution retirement plan, such as a nonqualified profit-sharing plan or matching contributions under a Section 401(k) plan. If the plan includes vesting requirements or other substantial risks of forfeiture, it can be designed to satisfy the short-term deferral rule. (See **Q. 17.**) If the short-term deferral rule does not apply but the plan complies with Section 409A and other law governing constructive receipt, in both form and operation, federal income tax will be deferred until actual or constructive receipt of deferred amounts as provided for under the plan.

Citation: ***See generally*** **26 USC Section 409A(a); Treasury Regulation Section 1.409A-1 – 3.**

Q.49. How are employer nonaccount balance plans treated under Section 409A?

Employer nonaccount balance plans are a separate plan type for purposes of Section 409A. (See **Q. 39.**) Typical employer nonaccount balance plans are nonqualified defined benefit pension plans that promise the employee monthly periodic payments for life or a specified period of time, rather than the amount accrued in an individual account. Entitlement to a benefit under such plans is commonly subject to vesting requirements and other substantial risks of forfeiture. If the plan includes vesting requirements or other substantial risks of forfeiture, it can be designed to satisfy the short-term deferral rule. (See **Q. 39.**) If the plan complies with Section 409A and other law governing constructive receipt, in both form and operation, federal income tax will be deferred until actual or constructive receipt of deferred amounts as provided for under the plan.

Citation: ***See generally*** **26 USC Section 409A(a); Treasury Regulation Section 1.409A-1 – 3.**

SERVICE PROVIDER ELECTIONS UNDER DEFERRED COMPENSATION PLANS SUBJECT TO SECTION 409A

Q.50. What types of service provider elections are typically provided under deferred compensation plans subject to Section 409A?

In a participant elective deferral account balance plan, the service provider must make a threshold election to defer the compensation rather than receive it on a current basis. This type of election is not appropriate for plans consisting solely of employer-provided benefits because the amounts accrued under such plans do not depend on the service provider's deferral of compensation.

In addition, participant elective deferral account balance plans typically provide for service provider elections respecting the time and form of payment. Plans consisting solely of employer-provided benefits may also provide for such elections. However, vest and pay plans do not provide for this type of election. (See **Q. 21**.) If a plan provides for service provider elections, Section 409A provides strict limits on the time of the initial election and subsequent changes (**Q. 51**).

Q.51. When must initial elections to defer and to designate the time and form of payment be made under Section 409A?

General Rule: In general, the service provider's initial election to defer compensation, including the amount deferred or the method of determining the amount deferred and the time and form of payment, must occur and must be irrevocable before the beginning of the taxable year (December 31 in the case of a calendar year) of the service provider in which the services relating to such compensation are to be rendered. The service recipient generally cannot retain any right to override these elections once they become irrevocable.

The following exceptions and limitations apply:

- *30-Day Rule for Newly-Eligible Participants:* A service provider that becomes eligible for deferred compensation for the first time after the general deadline for making elections with respect to a taxable year may make an initial election to defer within 30 days following the date of initial eligibility. The election may apply only to compensation earned after the date of the election. The controlled group and plan aggregation rules apply to determine a participant's first date of eligibility.

- *Deferral of Bonuses in the Case of a Mid-Year Start (Pro Rata Rule):* In the case of a newly eligible participant with a mid-year start, the deferred amount of any compensation based on a specified performance period (*e.g.*, an annual bonus) cannot exceed a pro rata portion of such compensation based on the remaining time in the performance period unless the compensation qualifies as performance-based compensation. For example, if an initial deferral election becomes effective on October 1, a participant may defer a maximum of 92/365ths or 25.2% of the participant's annual bonus for the calendar year.

- *Previously-Eligible Participants (Retirees and Transfers):* A service provider who has not been an active participant in any like-kind Section 409A plan for at least 24 months is subject to the initial eligibility rules. For this purpose, a service provider is an active participant in the plan if, under the plan's terms and without further amendment or action by the employer, the service provider is eligible to elect to defer compensation or otherwise accrue benefits under the plan other than earnings on prior deferrals.

- *Performance-Based Compensation:* Special rules apply to elections to defer performance-based compensation. (See **Q. 52** and **Exhibit 2.**)

- *Fiscal Year Plans:* If the compensation is payable on the basis of one or more of the service recipient's fiscal years, and if no part of such compensation is payable during such fiscal year(s), the initial elections may be made not later than the close of the prior fiscal year. For example, fiscal year compensation would include an annual bonus arrangement based on the employer's performance during its fiscal year ending September 30, 2011, provided that no part of the bonus is payable until after such fiscal year ends.

- *Sales Commissions:* For *bona fide* sales or renewal sales commissions, elections must be made before January 1 of the calendar year in which the customer remits payment for the services or product or, if applied consistently to all similarly situated service providers, the January 1 in which the sale occurs.

- *Investment Commissions:* For investment commissions based on the value of financial products, the services are deemed to be performed over the 12 months prior to the date on which the investment commission is determined, so the election must be made before January 1 of the calendar year in which the 12-month measuring period begins.

- *Annualized Recurring Part-year Compensation (Educator's Compensation):* For recurring part-year compensation of educators who have the right to elect to annualize their compensation over a 12-month period rather than the shorter period during which they render services (typically nine months), the arrangement will not be subject to Section 409A if the participant elects to annualize the recurring part-year compensation over a period not to exceed 13 months, and the election is made before the first day of the employment period. (See **Q. 53**.)

- *Evergreen Elections:* An evergreen election that remains in effect until and unless terminated or modified is permitted if it meets the Section 409A test for irrevocability each calendar year. For example, a plan could permissibly provide that a service provider's deferral election will remain in effect until changed or revoked, but that as of each December 31 such election will become irrevocable with respect to compensation earned in the following calendar year.

- *Excess Benefit Plans:* For excess benefit plans the sole purpose of which is to fund benefits in excess of the limits imposed on tax-qualified retirement plans under the Code, the initial election must be made not later than 30 days after the employee becomes eligible to participate. For this purpose, eligibility to participate occurs on the first day of the year immediately following the year in which the employee first accrues a benefit under the plan, and the initial election will apply to all benefits accrued under the plan before and after the election, unless and until an appropriate subsequent election is made. (See **Q. 54.**)

Because of the changing variable elements that apply in determining accruals under defined benefit excess benefit plans, it is possible that an employee would accrue a benefit in one year, have that benefit reduced to zero in a later year and have it increased in a still later year. In this case, the initial elections must be made when the employee first accrues a benefit, and all subsequent accruals under the plan are subject to that election.

Former participants who lose eligibility or terminate employment and subsequently regain eligibility to participate are also governed by this rule (Treas. Reg. § 1.409A-2(a)(7)).

- *Linked Plans:* As to nonqualified deferred compensation plans under which the amount deferred is determined in whole or in part by the benefits to be provided under a qualified pension plan, the following changes will not be deemed as either impermissible Section 409A elections or accelerations:

    - An increase or decrease in amounts deferred under the nonqualified deferred compensation plan that results directly from changes in the qualified plan limits imposed by the Code (*e.g.*, the limit on qualified plan compensation imposed by Code Section 401(a)(17));

    - The participant's actions or inactions under the qualified plan as to pre-tax elective deferrals that do not result in an increase or decrease in the amount deferred under the nonqualified deferred compensation plan by more than the Section 402(g)(1)(b) limits ($16,500 in 2010) in any calendar year; and

    - The participant's actions or inactions under the qualified plan as to pre-tax and after-tax elective deferrals that affect employer matching amounts or other contingent amounts credited under the nonqualified plan that do not exceed 100% of the matching or contingent amounts that would have been credited under the qualified plan in the absence of the qualified plan limitation (Treas. Reg. § 1.409A-(a)(9)).

- *Elections of Time and Form of Payment with Respect to Employer Plans:* If a plan does *not* permit a participant to elect to defer current compensation, as is typical of employer nonaccount balance plans, the plan may permit a participant to elect the time and form of payment by the latest date that the participant could have made a deferral election if such an election were available under the plan or the date that the service recipient grants a legally binding right to the compensation, whichever is later (Treas. Reg. § 1.409A-2(a)(1)).

- *Compensation Subject to Forfeiture:* If a participant's right to a payment under a plan is conditioned on continued future services for at least 12 months, the plan may permit the participant to elect to defer receipt of the payment within 30 days after the participant acquires a legally binding right to the payment (Treas. Reg. § 1.409A-2(a)(5)).

- *Deferral of Short-Term Deferral Awards prior to Vesting:* If a participant's right to a payment under the plan is subject to a substantial risk of forfeiture, the plan may permit the participant to elect to defer the payment if the election to defer is made at least 12 months before the date the substantial risk of forfeiture lapses and the date for payment specified in the election to defer is at least five years after the date of lapse of the substantial risk of forfeiture. For example, an employer grants an employee a bonus on January 1, 2008, payable on January 1, 2010, provided that the employee continues to be employed through January 1, 2010. The employee may elect to defer the compensation on or before January 1, 2009, so long as the election delays payment to January 1, 2015, or later (five years from the date the substantial risk of forfeiture lapses).

- *Plan Aggregation:* All plans of a controlled group that are of the same type for purposes of Section 409A are treated as a single plan for this purpose (see **Q. 39**), so all initial elections under all like-kind plans must occur within the same time period. *Some employers limit eligibility to participate and make initial elections under all plans maintained by the controlled group that are of the same type for this purpose to one or two 30-day window periods per year (for example, June and December) to be sure this requirement is satisfied.*

Citation: Treasury Regulation Section 1.409A-2(a).

Q.52. What is performance-based compensation for purposes of Section 409A?

Elections to defer performance-based compensation must be made by the earlier of six calendar months before the end of the performance period (for example, by June 30 in the case of a calendar year bonus performance period) or the date the performance-based compensation has become readily ascertainable. For this purpose, compensation is readily ascertainable to the extent it is certain to be paid.

The Section 409A regulations set forth the following principles for determining whether an amount constitutes performance-based compensation:

- The performance goals may be based upon individual or organizational criteria.
- The performance period must be at least 12 consecutive calendar months. Quarterly bonuses would not qualify.
- The participant must perform services continuously from the beginning of the performance period or the date the performance criteria are established, whichever is later, through the date of the election to defer.
- The performance goals must be communicated to the participant in writing within 90 days from the beginning of the performance period.
- Any performance-based compensation must be separately identified or designated under the plan.
- Compensation will not fail to constitute performance-based compensation merely because of a provision for automatic payment in the event of death, disability or a change in control.

- Compensation will fail to qualify as performance-based compensation as a result of a provision for automatic payment in the event of termination of employment irrespective of performance.

These requirements are similar but not identical to the requirements for performance-based compensation for purposes of Section 162(m). For example, neither Board nor shareholder approval is required for compensation to qualify as performance-based compensation under the Section 409A rules.

Citation: Treasury Regulation Section 1.409A-2(a)(8).

Q.53. Does a service provider's ability to elect that compensation earned in a 9- or 10- month period, typically an academic year, be paid over a 12-month period spanning two taxable years create nonqualified deferred compensation subject to Section 409A?

Yes. This pattern, typical to employees of academic institutions, is called *recurring part-year compensation*. For example, a school year starts August 1, 2010, and ends May 31, 2011 (10 months), and a teacher earns $5,400 per month ($54,000 per year). If the teacher were paid over 10 months, the teacher would receive $27,000 in 2010 for the five months of August through December, and $27,000 in 2011 for the following five months of January through May. If the teacher were paid over 12 months, the teacher would receive $4,500 per month, totaling $22,500 in 2010 for the five months of August through December and $31,500 in 2011 for the following seven months of January through July. As a result, $4,500 that the teacher earned in 2010 would be paid in 2011, so this amount would constitute nonqualified deferred compensation subject to Section 409A.

Is there an exception to the general rule of 409A coverage?

Yes. A service provider receiving regular recurring part-year compensation is excepted from compliance with both Section 409A and Section 457 if the compensation is not deferred beyond the last day of the 13th month following the beginning of the work period (for example, October 31 of the following year, if the school year begins on September 1 of the current year); and the amount of compensation deferred from one taxable year to the next does not exceed the Section 402(g)(1)(b) limit for the taxable year in which it is earned ($16,500 in 2010).

Example. The school year begins September 1, 2010, and ends June 30, 2011 (10 months), which means an employee will work four months in 2010 and six months in 2011. If the employee's base salary is $247,487, the employee will earn $98,995 in 2010 and $148,492 in 2011; however, based on a 12-month pay schedule, the employee will be paid approximately $82,495 in 2010 and $164,992 in 2011. The amount deferred is calculated by subtracting what the participant has actually been paid in 2010 from what the participant earned in that year: $98,995 - $82,495 = $16,500.

Note that this example makes it clear that the most a participant can earn and still claim the exception was $247,487 under the facts of the 2010 school year start and 2011 end. The maximum compensation that will qualify will change based upon the Section 402(g)(1)(b) limit for the year as well as when the school year begins and ends. In general, the earlier the school year starts, the lesser the maximum salary that will qualify for the exception. This calculation needs to be done each year, unless there is no change in any of the factors in the calculation for an employee.

What does Section 409A require if an election is offered?

The IRS has excepted regular recurring part-year compensation from the requirements of Section 409A. However, if this exception is not available, the general rules for elections to defer compensation under Section 409A apply, as follows:

- The teacher (or other participant) must give a written (or electronic) election to the employer that notifies the employer that the participant wants to spread out the compensation.
- The election must be made before the beginning of the work period (for example, before the first day of the school year for which the teacher is paid, which may be before the first day students arrive for class).
- The election must be irrevocable, so that it cannot be changed after the work period begins.
- The election must state how the compensation is going to be paid if the election is made (for example, ratably over the 12 months starting with the beginning of the school year).

No particular form is necessary for this election, and it does not have to be filed with the IRS.

What if an employee does not submit an election, or misses the deadline?

If an employee does not submit an election, or submits an election after the deadline, the employee must be paid in the same way as other employees who do not make an election.

If a school district provides for an election, must the election requirements be made in writing?

Yes, but Section 409A does not require any specific type of plan document. For example, if the teacher signed an election form with the required information, that would be sufficient. In addition, an election can be made electronically, such as by e-mail. Other rules, such as the inability to change the election and the deadlines for the election, can be provided in any other document, such as a participant handbook or school board rules and regulations.

Is an employee required to make this election every year?

No. An arrangement may provide that a pre-existing election will remain in place until the participant elects to change it. For example, a teacher may elect to receive salary over 12 months, and that election could remain in effect indefinitely until the teacher changes the election. However, any change in such an evergreen election must be made before the beginning of the school year to which the change applies. A change in the method of payment in the middle of a school year is not allowed.

Does Section 409A require that an employee be provided an election?

No. For example, a school district may provide that all teachers will have their pay spread over 12 months, without providing any election to the teachers. In that case, the election rules discussed below would not apply and no additional taxes would be imposed under Section 409A.

Will the IRS impose any additional taxes if a school district and its participants fail to meet the requirements of the Final Regulations for any school years beginning before 2008?

No. The IRS will not impose additional taxes for failure to meet the deferral election timing and written plan requirements with respect to the annualization of compensation for work periods or school years beginning before January 1, 2008. This relief applies only to compensation that qualifies for the timing rule in the regulations applicable to elections to annualize recurring part-year compensation, and only to the extent the compensation is paid on or before December 31, 2008.

Citation: IR 2007-142 (8-7-2007); Notice 2008-62, 2008-29 I.R.B., (7-21-2008).

Q.54. Can a participant make a subsequent election to change the time or form of payment specified in an earlier election?

Yes, if the plan allows for such subsequent elections. The subsequent election must be made at least 12 months before the payment date specified in the earlier election, the new payment date must be at least five calendar years after the payment date specified in the earlier election, and the subsequent election will have no force or effect if the participant separates from service within the 12 months beginning on the date of the subsequent election.

A subsequent election may apply to all or a specified portion of the amount subject to the earlier election. For example, a participant could make a subsequent election to further defer 50% of an account balance subject to an existing election for payment of the account in lump sum, and could also elect that the amount further deferred be paid in installments over a specified period of time rather than a lump sum. (See **Q. 51** regarding time and form of payment.)

Also, a mere change of form of payment from one type of annuity to another actuarially equivalent annuity (using reasonable assumptions) that commences at the same time is not subject to the requirements of the subsequent election rule.

Citation: *See generally* Treasury Regulation Section 1.409A-2(b), and specifically 1.409A-2(b)(2) as to the definition of "payment"; *see* Treasury Regulation Section 1.409A-2(b)(ii) regarding elections to change the form of annuity payment.

Q.55. Can a participant cancel an election to defer compensation during the plan year in which the compensation would otherwise have been paid absent the election?

Generally not. The following exceptions apply:

- An election to defer may be changed or terminated for the remaining portion of the year if the participant becomes disabled (see **Q. 27**) or takes an unforeseeable emergency distribution during the year. (See **Q. 30.**) A plan sponsor may require a cancellation of the elected deferrals under a nonqualified plan for the balance of the year based upon (i) a 409A unforeseeable emergency or (ii) the grant of a qualified plan hardship distribution under Treas. Reg. § 1.401(k)-1(d)(3)(iv). In the case of a cancellation for reason of an unforeseeable emergency, the cancellation of the deferral election must be for the remainder of the entire relevant plan year. Note: This ability to cancel the nonqualified plan elective deferral under Code Section 409A is important in order to permit a financial hardship distribution under a qualified Section 401(k) plan, since qualified plan law only permits the distribution if the financial need cannot be met by plan loans or ceasing deferrals under other qualified or nonqualified plans.

- An election may be changed or terminated if the election pertains to performance-based compensation (see **Q. 52**) and the deadline for making the election has not yet occurred.

Citation: *See generally* 26 USC Section 409A(a)(A)-(B) and specifically 26 USC Section 409A(a)(4)(b)(iii); also *See generally* Treasury Regulation Section 1.409A-2(a)(1) and (8); also 1.409A-3(j)(4)(vii) and (xiii). *Also See* Preamble to Proposed 409A Regulations, Section VII.D. as to unforeseeable emergency distributions.

Q.56. Can a plan permit a service provider to make multiple elections among distribution forms?

Yes. The distribution rules apply separately to each identifiable amount payable on a determinable date. A plan may create multiple separate accounts for a service provider each of which can be governed by a separate election.

Q.57. Can a plan provide that distribution will occur on the earliest of two or more permissible events?

Yes. A plan may provide that a benefit or account will be distributed at the earliest of several permissible distribution events, such as separation from service, death, disability, change in control or unforeseeable emergency. The plan may provide for a different form of payment with respect to each such distribution event. However, with respect to any one of these permissible distribution events, payments must generally all be made in the same manner. For example, a plan may not provide for one time and form of payment if a separation from service occurs on a Monday and another form and time of payment if a separation from service occurs on any other day of the week. This prohibition against use of different forms of payment with respect to a specific triggering event is sometimes referred to as the rule prohibiting "toggling" among different payment methods.

Notwithstanding the "anti-toggling rule" described in the preceding paragraph, a plan may allow for an alternative payment schedule with respect to any of the distribution events described above if the event occurs on or before one (but not more than one) specified date. For example, a plan may provide that a service provider will receive a lump sum payment of the service provider's entire benefit under the plan on the first day of the month following a change in control event that occurs before the service provider attains age 55, but will receive five substantially equal annual payments commencing on the first day of the month following a change in control event that occurs on or after the service provider attains age 55.

In the case of a plan that provides for payment upon separation from service, a different time and form of payment may be designated with respect to a separation from service under each of the following conditions:

- A separation from service during a limited period of time not to exceed two years following a change in control event;
- A separation from service before or after a specified date (including the attainment of a specified age), or a separation from service before or after a combination of a specified date and completion of a specified number of years of service (for example, attaining age 55 and completing 10 years of service); and
- A separation from service not described in the first two bullet points above.

The drafters of the regulations have made it very clear that a third "toggle" is not permitted. For example, a plan may not provide for a different payment form upon voluntary versus involuntary termination of employment.

Example. A plan provides that an individual will receive a lump sum payment of benefits upon separation from service within two years after a change in control, or payments in the form of 15 annual installments upon separation from service after attainment of age 55 and completion of ten years of service, or a payment in the form of five annual installments upon separation from service for any other reason. This plan design is considered to have two "toggles" which satisfy the "anti-toggling" rule.

Citation: Treasury Regulation Section 1.409A-2(b)(2)(i); Treasury Regulation Section 1.409A-3(c); ABA Section of Taxation, Joint Committee on Participant Benefits, May Meeting 2009, May 7-9, pp. 15-16; Annotated Regulations documenting the comments of Stephen Tackney at the ABA Section of Taxation meeting held on May 9, 2008 ("You cannot have a different form of payment based on marital status, *i.e.*, a joint and survivor annuity if the participant is married, but a lump sum payment if the participant is single; there can be different forms of actuarially equivalent annuities, which will be treated as one time and form of payment, provided the beginning date for the payment does not change"), the comments of Stephen Tackney at the ALI-ABA Section 409A Compliance and Drafting Challenges Webcast held on February 4, 2008 ("I stress . . . you can't come up with a third independent toggle that isn't age and service or change in control"), the comments of Helen Morrison at the ALI-ABA Section 409A Compliance and Drafting Challenges Webcast held on February 4, 2008 (A third toggle permitting you to have a different payment for voluntary versus involuntary termination "doesn't work"), and the comments of Daniel Hogans at the Steptoe & Johnson audio conference held on May 1, 2007 ("There is no toggle between involuntary and voluntary termination; that is

something you cannot do with deferred compensation anymore"), all reproduced immediately following Treasury Regulation Section 1.409A-3(c).

Q.58. Can benefits in pay status under a deferred compensation plan subject to Section 409A be suspended if an employee is rehired after a separation from service and resumes eligibility under the plan on resumption of employment?

The preamble to the final regulations takes the position that suspension of payment is not possible. In practice, the employee could defer additional compensation earned after employment resumes, live off the deferred compensation payments, and achieve an equivalent result.

Citation: Preamble to the Final 409A Regulations, § II.C.2.e. "Rehires and Suspension of Benefits."

Q.59. Can the subsequent election rule be used to increase participant flexibility in a plan with multiple annual election options?

Yes. The plan must provide for subsequent elections to delay distribution. Under this design, a participant could make fixed date elections to defer (for example, in anticipation of a child's expected college expenses), and if the participant finds that the elected distribution is not needed, the participant could make a subsequent election at least 12 months prior to the elected distribution date to delay distribution for an additional five years or more.

Note: As a practical matter, the plan administrator must be able to manage the complex accounting for this type of rolling deferral.

Citation: ***See generally*** **Treasury Regulation Section 1.409A-2(b)(1).**

Q.60. Can the subsequent election rule and the single or multiple payment election be used in combination to increase the security of benefits accrued under a participant individual account plan benefit?

Yes. The plan must provide for distribution in installments on a fixed date, treatment of each installment in a series as an individual payment, and subsequent elections to delay distribution. Under this regime, a participant could make an election before the beginning of each year to defer compensation earned during the year for two years and elect that the deferred amount be paid in the form of five annual installments. (See Chart 1 below.) At the end of year 1 and each subsequent year, the participant could make a subsequent election to defer distribution of the next scheduled installment payment for an additional five years. (See Chart 2.) If the participant determined for any reason that additional deferrals were no longer appropriate, the participant would discontinue all elections to defer, including new deferrals and subsequent elections. This would cause distribution to begin during the next year and be complete within five years.

Note: The plan administrator must be able to manage the accounting for this type of rolling deferral.

Chart 1: Participant elects a two-year fixed date deferral to be paid in five annual installments.

Tax Year	Elected Deferral Amount	Scheduled Distribution Amount	Distribution Date
2010	$50,000	$0	
2011		$0	
2012		$10,000	Jan. 8
2013		$10,000	Jan. 8
2014		$10,000	Jan. 8
2015		$10,000	Jan. 8
2016		$10,000	Jan. 8

Chart 2: Participant subsequently elects to push back the first installment five years to the end of the sequence of installments. This subsequent election is repeated every year as desired.

Tax Year	Prior Elected Distribution Schedule	5-Year Re-Deferral	Revised Distribution Schedule
2011			
2012	$10.000		
2013	$10.000		$10.000
2014	$10.000		$10.000
2015	$10.000		$10.000
2016	$10.000		$10.000
2017		$10.000	$10.000

Citation: *See generally* Treasury Regulation Section 1.409A-2(b)(1); *see specifically* 1.409A-2(b)(2)(i) as to single or multiple "payments" (and the definitions of payments generally).

SEVERANCE PLANS

Q.61. What severance payments are exempt from Section 409A?

Severance payments that are payable solely on involuntary termination of employment or termination for good reason (as defined in **Q. 64**) and that are paid in their entirety within the short-term deferral period are exempt from Section 409A under the short-term deferral rule.

If severance payments do not qualify as short-term deferrals, they will nonetheless be exempt from Section 409A to the extent they satisfy the requirements of the following separate rules governing severance pay plans:

- The severance payments must occur only on involuntary separation from service, voluntary separation for good reason (**Q. 63**) or pursuant to a window program (**Q. 67**),
- The severance payments cannot exceed two times the participant's annualized compensation for the year before the separation or two times the maximum limit on compensation taken into account under a tax-qualified retirement plan pursuant to Section 401(a)(17) for the year

of separation (for 2010, the Section 401(a)(17) limitation is $245,000, and two times this limit would therefore be $490,000), and

- Payment must be made by the end of the second calendar year following the year the participant separates from service.

Citation: Treasury Regulation Sections 1.409A-1(b)(4) and 1.409A-1(b)(9).

Q.62. When designing a severance pay program that is intended to be exempt from Section 409A, must the architect of the plan choose between the short-term deferral rule and the severance plan rules, or can both rules be applied in combination?

Both of these rules can be used in combination to maximize the amounts exempt from Section 409A if the documentation is drafted appropriately. To accomplish this, each payment in a series of severance payments must be designated in writing as a separate payment for purposes of Section 409A. Then the payments made within the short-term deferral period will fall outside the scope of Section 409A under the short-term deferral rule, and the remaining payments will qualify as involuntary separation pay to the extent such payments satisfy the limits on the amount and time of payment. (See **Q. 63.**)

Example. An executive with base compensation of $30,000 per month has an employment agreement that promises two years of salary continuation payments following the executive's involuntary termination from employment without cause. The executive's employment is involuntarily terminated without cause on June 30, 2010, and severance payments begin on July 1, 2010, in the amount of $30,000 per month. If the employment agreement provides that each monthly severance payment is considered a separate payment for purposes of Section 409A, then the first nine severance payments (from July 1, 2010, through March 1, 2011) will be exempt from Section 409A under the short-term deferral rule because they will be made within 2½ months after the close of the calendar year of severance. The remaining 15 monthly severance payments, totaling $450,000, are exempt from Section 409A under the severance pay rules, because the total amount is less than two times the Section 401(a)(17) limit for 2010 and all payments are completed by the end of the second calendar year following the year of termination. If the plan had not provided that each installment is treated as a separate payment, the entire benefit would have been treated as one; it would not have been subject to the short-term deferral exception because payment would not have been completed within 2½ months after the year of termination; the exempt amount would have been limited to two times the Section 401(a)(17) limit for 2010, or $490,000; and the payments in excess of that amount, or $270,000, would have been subject to the Section 409A requirements.

To the extent that severance pay may not be excluded from Section 409A's application under a combination of the short-term deferral rule and severance plan rules, the Final Regulations offer an additional exclusion from the ambit of Section 409A for limited payments. To the extent not otherwise excluded, the parties to a separation pay arrangement may treat a right to a payment as not providing for a deferral of compensation to the extent such payment does not exceed the applicable dollar limitation under Section 402(g)(1)(B) ($16,500 for 2010) for the year of the separation from service. Accordingly, short-term deferrals, payments exempt from Section 409A under the separation pay rules, and limited payments described in the preceding sentence may be used in combination to exclude the maximum amount of separation pay from the application of Section 409A.

Citation: Treasury Regulation Sections 1.409A-1(b)(4)(i)(F) and 1.409A-1(b)(9)(v)(D).

Q.63. Can severance amounts payable on account of voluntary termination or termination for good reason qualify as severance pay for purposes of Section 409A?

In general, severance pay available on either voluntary or involuntary termination of employment does not qualify for the severance pay exemption from Section 409A. Moreover, such severance pay would not be considered subject to a substantial risk of forfeiture because it could be payable upon voluntary termination of employment, and therefore would not qualify for the short-term deferral exception to Section 409A. However, in certain circumstances, an employee's decision to terminate employment for good reason as defined in the plan may be treated as if it were an involuntary severance for purposes of the severance pay rule and short-term deferral rule.

Citation: Treasury Regulation Sections 1.409A-1(b)(9)(iii) and 1.409A-1(n).

Q.64. When is termination for good reason considered equivalent to involuntary severance?

The regulations include a safe harbor definition of good reason for this purpose. The safe harbor requires the following:

- The separation from service must occur during a pre-determined period of time not to exceed two years following the initial existence of one or more of the following conditions arising without the consent of the participant:
    - A material diminution in the participant's base compensation
    - A material diminution in the participant's authority duties, or responsibilities
    - A material diminution in the authority, duties, or responsibilities of the supervisor to whom the participant is required to report, including a requirement that the participant report to a corporate officer or employee instead of reporting directly to the board of directors of a corporation
    - A material diminution in the budget over which the participant retains authority
    - A material change in the geographic location at which the participant must perform the services

- Any other action or inaction that constitutes a material breach by the employer of the agreement under which the participant provides services

- The amount, time and form of payment upon separation from service must be substantially identical to the amount, time and form of payment payable due to an involuntary separation from service, to the extent such a right exists.

- The participant must be required to provide notice to the employer of the existence of a condition giving rise to good reason no later than 90 days after the initial existence of the condition, and the employer must be provided a cure period of at least 30 days.

This is only a safe harbor. Other good reason definitions may be deemed equivalent to involuntary severance based on all of the facts and circumstances. The facts and circumstances must include employer actions resulting in a material negative change to the employee in the employer-employee relationship, such as the duties to be performed, the conditions under which the duties are to be performed, or the compensation to be received for performing the services. Other factors include (i) the extent to which the payments are in the same amount and are to be made at the same time and in the same form as payments available upon involuntary severance, (ii) whether the employee is required to give the employer notice of the existence of the condition that would result in treatment as a separation from service for good reason, and (iii) whether the employer has a reasonable right to cure.

Citation: Treasury Regulation Section 1.409A-1(n)(2).

Q.65. If all payments due under a severance arrangement do not meet the short-term deferral exception or the separation pay exception, does a violation of Section 409A occur?

If all or some portion of severance pay does not fit within one of these exceptions, it is subject to Section 409A but is not necessarily in breach of Section 409A. If the plan meets all of the requirements of Section 409A in both form and operation, there is no breach. This requires that the arrangement clearly specify the form and time of payment; that the form and time of payment not be changed after the schedule is established; and, in the case of a public company, that any payments to specified employees be delayed for at least six months following separation.

Citation: 26 USC Section 409A(a)(1)(a)(i); Treasury Regulation Section 1.409-1(c)(1)-(3).

Q.66. Can severance payments be made in substitution for nonqualified deferred compensation payments that are being forfeited?

No. Any payment or benefit, including severance pay, that is a substitute for or replacement of amounts deferred under a separate nonqualified deferred compensation plan is treated as payment of the compensation deferred under the separate nonqualified deferred compensation plan **(Q. 34)**.

Example. An executive is terminated before age 65 and as a result forfeits the right to receive a nonqualified pension payment commencing at age 65. If the executive receives a lump sum severance payment equal to the present value of the forfeited benefit, the severance payment is treated as an accelerated payment of the forfeited benefit in violation of Section 409A.

If an employee receives a severance payment at separation from service and also has a legally binding but forfeitable right to deferred compensation payable at a future date that is forfeited on account of the separation from service, whether or not the severance payment is treated as a substitute for the amount forfeited is based on the facts and circumstances. If the separation from service is voluntary, it is presumed that the severance payment is a substitute for the forfeited amount in breach of Section 409A. The presumption may be rebutted by a demonstration that the employee would have obtained the severance payment regardless of the forfeiture.

Citation: Treasury Regulation Section 1.409A-1(b)(9)(i).

Q.67. What is a window program for purposes of the exception to Section 409A for severance pay?

A window program is a program established by an employer to provide severance for a window period not in excess of 12 months under which the employer pays special severance pay to employees who separate from service during the window period. A program will not be considered a window program if the employer establishes a pattern of repeatedly providing for similar separation pay in similar circumstances for substantially consecutive periods.

Citation: Treasury Regulation Section 1.409A-1(b)(9)(vi).

Q.68. Do collectively bargained severance plans and foreign severance plans required by local law get special treatment?

Yes. They are exempt from Section 409A's requirements *per se*.

Citation: Treasury Regulation Sections 1.409A-1(m) and (n)(2); Treasury Regulation Section 1.409A-1(b)(9)(i)-(iv).

STOCK-BASED COMPENSATION

Q.69. Does Section 409A apply to nonstatutory stock options and stock appreciation rights ("SARs")?

Nonqualified stock options and SARs are within the scope of Section 409A because they afford the service provider a legally binding right to compensation that will be realized in a later taxable year. However, the final regulations provide that nonqualified stock options and SARs can be structured to avoid Section 409A treatment, as follows:

With respect to nonqualified stock options:

- The stock subject to the option must constitute "service recipient stock" (**Q. 70** and **Q. 71**);
- The option exercise price cannot be less than the fair market value of the underlying stock on the date the option is granted;
- The number of shares subject to the option must be fixed on the date of grant;
- The transfer or exercise of the option must be subject to taxation under Section 83 and Treasury Regulation Section 1.83-7; and
- The option cannot include any feature for deferral of compensation other than the deferral of recognition of income until the later of the date of exercise or disposition, or the date the stock acquired pursuant to the option exercise first becomes substantially vested.

With respect to stock appreciation rights:

- The stock subject to the SAR must constitute "service recipient stock" (**Q. 70** and **Q. 71**));
- The SAR exercise price cannot be less than the fair market value of the underlying service recipient stock on the date of grant;
- The number of shares subject to the SAR must be fixed on the date of grant;
- The compensation payable under the SAR cannot be greater than the excess of the fair market value of the service recipient stock on the date the SAR is exercised over an amount specified in the SAR documents on the date of grant (the "SAR exercise price"); and
- The SAR must not include any feature for the deferral of compensation other than the deferral of recognition of income until the SAR is exercised.

For example, a nonstatutory option or SAR that permits the service provider to elect to defer receipt of the compensation otherwise payable on exercise until termination of employment would not satisfy these requirements, and would cause the option or SAR to be subject to Section 409A.

However, neither the right to receive nonvested stock upon the exercise of a stock right nor the right to pay the exercise price with previously acquired shares constitutes a feature for the deferral of compensation for this purpose.

Citation: Treasury Regulation Section 1.409A-1(b)(5).

Q.70. What constitutes service recipient stock for purposes of the exception to Section 409A for stock-based compensation?

Service recipient stock generally means common stock of a corporation that employs a service provider or a direct or indirect "parent" of such employer, looking at the line of ownership only in an upward direction. Liquidation preferences are permitted, but dividend preferences are not. The ownership threshold for each parent or sub-parent, when looking in such upward direction, is 50% or, if justified by legitimate business criteria, as low as 20%.

Example. An employee works for Corporation C, which is 50% owned by Corporation A and 50% owned by Corporation B. Neither Corporation A nor Corporation B are related. Service recipient stock with respect to the employee would include common stock of either Corporation A, Corporation B or Corporation C.

For this purpose, whether or not criteria are legitimate business criteria is based on all the facts and circumstances. There must be a sufficient nexus between the service provider and the issuer of the option or SAR such that the grant serves a legitimate non-tax business purpose. Avoidance of Section 409A is not a sufficient nexus. For example, stock options of a corporation that owns an interest in a joint venture that is an operating business granted to service providers of the joint venture who formerly were employees of the issuer or who the issuer reasonably expects will become employees of the issuer in the future generally will constitute use of service recipient stock based on legitimate business criteria, so long as the issuer owns at least 20% of the joint venture. However, if a service provider has no real nexus with a corporate issuer, such as generally happens when the corporate issuer is the passive investor in the service recipient joint venture, an option or SAR issued to that employee with respect to the corporation's stock generally would not be based on legitimate business criteria.

Service recipient stock does not include stock that is subject to a mandatory repurchase obligation (other than a right of first refusal) or a put or call right that is not a lapse restriction as defined in Treasury Regulation Section 1.83-3(i) if the purchase price is based on a measure other than the fair market value of the issuer's stock. For example, if an option is issued with an exercise price equal to fair market value of the issuer's stock on the date of grant, but the service provider must sell the stock received on exercise at termination of employment based on a formula price equal to two times the issuer's book value on the date of the sale, the book value formula is not necessarily based on fair market value, so the option would not satisfy this requirement and it would be subject to Section 409A.

Q.71. How is fair market value of service recipient stock determined for purposes of determining the exercise price of an option or SAR?

For stock that is readily tradable on an established securities market, the fair market value of the stock is based on market price. Fair market value may be based on the last sale before or the first sale after the grant, the closing price on the trading day before the trading day of the grant, the average of the high and low prices on the trading day before or the trading day of the grant, or any other reasonable method using actual transactions with respect to such stock as reported by the established securities market. An average selling price may be used if the employer designates the recipient of the stock right; the number and class of shares of stock that are subject to the stock right; and the method for determining the exercise price, including the period over which the averaging will occur, before the beginning of the specified averaging period. The averaging period cannot exceed 30 days before or after the grant date.

For stock that is not readily tradable on an established securities market, fair market value can be determined by reasonable application of a reasonable valuation method, based on all the facts and circumstances, including the value of company's tangible and intangible assets, the present value of its anticipated future cash flows, the market value of stock or equity interests in similar businesses, recent arm's-length sales or transfer of the stock, control premiums or discounts for lack of marketability, and whether the valuation method is used for other purposes that have a material economic effect on the employer, its stockholders, or its creditors. The use of a valuation method is not reasonable if it fails to take into consideration all available material information. For example, the use of a prior valuation that does not take into account information that became available at a later time and may materially affect the value of the company, such as resolution of material litigation or issuance of a patent, would not be reasonable. A valuation as of a date more than 12 months before the grant date is not reasonable. The employer's consistent use of a valuation method for other purposes unrelated to compensation of service providers tends to support its reasonableness.

Any of the following valuation methods is presumed reasonable, subject to rebuttal by the IRS upon a showing that either the valuation method or its application was grossly unreasonable:

- A valuation determined by an independent appraisal as of a date not more than 12 months before the grant date.

- A formula valuation that satisfies the requirements of Treasury Regulation Section 1.83-5, if the same method is used for purposes of any transfer of shares of the same class or a substantially similar class to the company or the owner of more than 10% of the total combined voting power of all classes of stock of the company, other than an arm's-length transaction involving the sale of all or substantially all of the outstanding stock, provided the valuation method is used consistently for all purposes.

- A valuation made reasonably and in good faith and evidenced by a written report that takes into account the relevant factors with respect to illiquid stock of a start-up corporation. For this purpose, a start-up corporation means a corporation that has conducted business for less than 10 years and has no stock that is readily tradable on an established security market. This methodology is not available if the service recipient or service provider may reasonably anticipate, as of the time of the grant, that the service recipient will undergo a change in control event within the 90 days following the grant date or make a public offering of securities within 180 days following the grant date. A valuation will not be considered made reasonably and in good faith unless the valuation is performed by a person or persons that the corporation reasonably determines is qualified to perform such a valuation based on the person's or persons' significant knowledge, experience, education or training. For this purpose, significant experience generally means at least five years of relevant experience in business valuation or appraisal, financial accounting, investment banking, private equity, secured lending, or other comparable experience in the line of business or industry in which the service recipient operates.

A different valuation method may be used for each grant, but a single valuation method must be used for each separate action and cannot be changed retroactively. For example, one valuation method may be used to establish the exercise price of the stock option, and a different valuation method may be used to determine the value at the date of the repurchase of stock pursuant to a put or call right, but once established, the exercise price or amount to be paid cannot be changed through the retroactive use of another valuation method.

Representatives of the Internal Revenue Service and the Treasury have stated that the government is not going to use hindsight to judge a valuation method. Taking all relevant facts into account, if the taxpayer comes up with a valuation number, the Internal Revenue Service will be evaluating the taxpayer on its application of the method, not whether the taxpayer "got the number exactly right."

Citation: Treasury Regulation Section 1.409A-1(b)(5)(iv); Annotated Regulations documenting the comments of Daniel Hogans at the NASPP webcast on April 16, 2007, reproduced in bold letters immediately following Treasury Regulation Section 1.409A-1(b)(5)(iv)(B)(2); Annotated Regulations documenting the comments of Daniel Hogans at the PriceWaterhouseCoopers webcast held on April 18, 2007, reproduced in bold letters immediately following Treasury Regulation Section 1.409A-1(b)(5)(iv)(B)(2)(iii).

Q.72. Can the exercise price be extended or the option or SAR modified without causing loss of the exception from Section 409A coverage?

A change in the terms of a stock right is generally considered to constitute the grant of a new stock right. The new stock right may or may not constitute a deferral of compensation under the principles described in Question 69 based on the facts and circumstances as of the deemed grant date of the new stock right. For this purpose, a change in terms of a stock right includes any change in the terms of the stock right itself and any change in the terms of the plan pursuant to which the stock right was granted or in the terms of any other agreement governing the stock right that may directly or indirectly reduce the exercise price, regardless of whether the holder in fact benefits from the change in terms.

In general, an extension of the exercise period constitutes an additional deferral feature that causes the option to be treated as an arrangement providing for the deferral of compensation from the original grant date, thus causing a violation of Section 409A. This rule does not apply if the extension occurs when the exercise price equals or exceeds the fair market value of underlying stock at the time of the extension or if the stock right is extended to the earlier of the date the original exercise period could have expired or the tenth anniversary of the original grant date.

A change shortening the exercise period is not a change for this purpose. Addition of a provision enabling tender of previously acquired stock for the stock available under the stock right or a provision enabling withholding shares of stock to facilitate payment of the exercise price or the employment taxes or required withholding taxes resulting from the exercise of the stock right is not a change for this purpose.

Citation: Treasury Regulation Section 1.409A-1(b)(5)(v).

Q.73. Does Section 409A apply to incentive stock options, or to options issued under employee stock purchase plans?

Incentive stock options under Section 422 and options granted under an employee stock purchase plan as described in Section 423 are generally exempt from the application of Section 409A. However, this exemption does not apply to a modification, extension or renewal of a statutory option that is treated as the grant of a new option that is not qualified under Section 422 or 423. In the case of such a modification, extension or renewal, the option is treated as if it had been a nonstatutory stock option from the date of the original grant.

Citation: Treasury Regulation Section 1.409A-1(b)(5)(ii).

Q.74. Does Section 409A apply to restricted stock, restricted stock units, or phantom stock units?

Restricted stock is stock issued subject to a substantial risk of forfeiture. Because the issuance of restricted stock by a service recipient to a service provider involves a transfer of property, Section 409A does not apply.

A restricted stock unit is a bookkeeping entry representing the value of one share of stock subject to vesting requirements. A restricted stock unit may be settled in cash at the time of vesting or shortly thereafter. If settlement occurs within 2½ months after the close of the year of vesting, the restricted stock unit will be a short-term deferral outside the scope of Section 409A. (See **Q. 17.**) If settlement occurs more than 2½ months after the close of the year of vesting, for example, if settlement occurs at termination of employment, then the restricted stock unit is subject to Section 409A and must be structured to comply with Section 409A.

A phantom stock unit is a bookkeeping entry representing the value of one share of stock similar to a restricted stock unit, but a phantom stock unit may or may not have a vesting requirement. A phantom stock unit subject to a vesting requirement is treated the same as a restricted stock unit for purposes of Section 409A. If a phantom stock unit has no vesting requirement, the short-term deferral rule cannot apply, and the phantom stock unit is subject to Section 409A and must be structured to comply with Section 409A.

Citation: Treasury Regulation Section 1.409A-1(b)(6)(i).

EMPLOYMENT AGREEMENTS

Q.75. Which common provisions of an employment agreement might create issues under Section 409A?

Employment agreements present subtle issues under Section 409A. Affected provisions may include the following:

- Severance (**Q. 61-68**)

- Equity awards (**Q. 69-72**)
- Nonqualified deferred compensation arrangements
- Tax gross-up payments (**Q. 77**)
- Offset of the employer's obligation to make payments due the employee by amounts the employee owes the employer (**Q. 34**)
- Continued coverage under self-insured medical plans following termination (**Q. 76**)
- In-kind or other reimbursement arrangements that continue after termination, such as continued use of a corporate jet or entitlement to reimbursement for financial planning services (**Q. 76**)
- Bonus provisions
- Releases (**Q. 28, Example 2**)

Citation: ***See generally*** **Treasury Regulation Sections 1.409A-1(b)(4) and 1.409A-1(b)(9).**

Q.76. What issues do fringe benefit arrangements pose under Section 409A?

Section 409A potentially applies to any taxable payment made in a year following the year in which the legally binding right to receive the payment arises. Section 409A is not limited to cash payments, but can include in-kind benefits such as the right to use a corporate jet or a company car.

The Final Regulations provide guidance on structuring taxable reimbursements and in-kind benefits to comply with Section 409A. Insured post-employment health benefits are not subject to Section 409A. A service provider's reimbursed medical expenses during the COBRA coverage period that are allowable as a deduction under Code Section 213 (disregarding the provision that expenses must exceed 7.5% of adjusted gross income) are not subject to Section 409A. Expenses must be incurred during the actual coverage period, which may be the maximum COBRA coverage period or any shorter period. Any other post-employment medical reimbursement is subject to Section 409A.

In general, reimbursements taxable to a service provider after separation from service and deductible by the service recipient and reasonable outplacement expenses are not subject to Section 409A if they are incurred not later than the end of the second taxable year following separation and reimbursed not later than the end of the third year following separation. This exception applies to such payments and reimbursements, even if the service provider is entitled to such reimbursements for expenses incurred after the end of this exempt period. Nontaxable benefits generally are also not covered by Section 409A.

Other fringe benefit and reimbursement arrangements are generally subject to Section 409A and are deemed to comply with Section 409A if the following requirements are met:

- For cash reimbursements of covered expenses, the arrangement must be in writing and must provide for reimbursement of expenses incurred during an objectively-prescribed period.

- The amount of reimbursable expenses incurred or in-kind benefits available in one taxable year cannot affect the amount of reimbursable expenses or in-kind benefits available in a different taxable year. For example, an employment agreement provision that the employee can be reimbursed for up to $30,000 in financial planning expenses during the first three years following separation from service would violate Section 409A because the use of the benefits in one calendar year would reduce the availability of the benefits in a different calendar year.

- The reimbursement arrangement must specify that payment must be made by no later than the end of participant's taxable year following the taxable year in which the expense is incurred.

- The right to reimbursement or in-kind benefits cannot be subject to liquidation or exchange for another benefit.

Citation: Treasury Regulation Section 1.409A-1(b)(9)(v); Treasury Regulation Section 1.409A-3(i)(1)(iv).

Q.77. Is a provision in an employment agreement for a tax gross-up payment (*e.g.*, to compensate an executive for golden parachute taxes) permitted under Section 409A?

Yes, if the agreement provides that the gross-up payment must be made by the end of the calendar year following the year in which the participant remits the related taxes to the government. A right to reimbursement for expenses associated with a tax audit or litigation addressing the existence or amount of a tax liability is permitted if the agreement requires that payment be made and payment is in fact made by the end of the calendar year following the calendar year in which the taxes subject to the audit or litigation are remitted to the government, or if no taxes are due as a consequence of the audit or litigation, the end of the calendar year following the calendar year in which the audit is completed or there is a final and non-appealable settlement or other resolution of the litigation.

Citation: Treasury Regulation Section 1.409A-3(i)(1)(v).

Q.78. Are payments made in settlement of litigation with an employer or payments made under indemnification agreements or directors and officers insurance treated as nonqualified deferred compensation subject to Section 409A?

No.

Legal Settlements: Section 409A generally does not apply to an employer's payment of settlement or award amounts that result from the resolution of a bona fide legal claim based on a wrongful termination, employment discrimination, the Fair Standards Labor Act or workers' compensation laws. This is true regardless if the claim arose under federal, state, local or foreign laws, and whether or not the amounts are treated as compensation for federal income tax purposes. However, this exception applies only to bona fide claims, not payment of any pre-existing deferred compensation subject to Section 409A that is restructured to be part of a legal settlement or award resolving the dispute, or payments in exchange for a waiver and release of claims unless the amounts paid relate to an actual bona fide claim for damages under applicable law.

Indemnification Payments: Section 409A does not apply to indemnification or directors and officers' insurance payments for damages or expenses incurred in connection with bona fide legal claims against the service provider in connection with the service provider's rendition of services, to the extent the right to indemnification is permissible under applicable law.

Citation: Treasury Regulation Section 1.409A-1(b)(10)-(11)

SPLIT-DOLLAR AND OTHER LIFE INSURANCE ARRANGEMENTS

Q.79. Which split-dollar life insurance arrangements are subject to or exempt from Section 409A coverage?

The regulations provide that the statutory exemption for death benefit plans is limited to the residual death benefit in a nonqualified deferred compensation plan. Compensatory split-dollar life insurance plans do not fall within this exemption, and they are generally subject to Section 409A.

A split-dollar arrangement is any arrangement between an owner and nonowner of a life insurance contract under which:

- Either party to the arrangement pays, either directly or indirectly, all or any portion of the premiums on a life insurance contract, including a payment by means of a loan to the other party that is secured by the life insurance contract;
- At least one of the parties to the arrangement paying premiums is entitled to recover (either conditionally or unconditionally) all or any portion of those premiums from the proceeds of the life insurance contract; and
- The arrangement is not a part of a group term life insurance plan described in Code Section 79.

In addition, regardless of the criteria above, a compensatory arrangement under which the employer pays any part of the premium is treated as a split-dollar arrangement.

Only two types of split-dollar life insurance arrangements are exempt from Section 409A: employer-owned endorsement split-dollar policies that provide only an interest in the policy's death proceeds to the non-owner employee (on the basis that they constitute bona fide death benefit plans); and loan split-dollar policies (on the basis that a loan does not involve deferral of compensation for purposes of Section 409A). In the case of a loan, minimum interest rates must be charged and paid by the employee.

Independent of the requirements of Section 409A, giving a participant a current interest in a split-dollar life insurance policy's cash values, unless the arrangement is a true loan, results in annual income taxation of the increase in cash value to the participant.

Citation: Notice 2007-34, 2007-17 I.R.B. (4-23-2007); *also see* Treasury Regulation Sections 1.61-22 and 1.7872-15.

Q.80. Are split-dollar life insurance programs subject to grandfathering under Section 409A?

If a split-dollar arrangement was entered into on or before October 3, 2004, whatever its form, contributions before January 1, 2005, and cash value attributable to those contributions are not subject to Section 409A unless the plan is materially modified after October 3, 2004. Pre-existing split-dollar life insurance plans with grandfathered and nongrandfathered amounts could be materially modified to comply with 2003 rules governing split-dollar arrangements without constituting a material modification for purposes of Section 409A.

The grandfathered portion can be calculated by use of any reasonable method that allocates increases in cash value attributable to premiums earned and vested on or before December 31, 2004. However, a method that disproportionately allocates costs and expenses to the nongrandfathered portion will not be deemed reasonable.

Citation: Notice 2007-34, 2007-17 I.R.B. 996 (4-23-2007).

Q.81. What is a bonus life insurance or annuity plan, and how can it be used as a substitute for a nonqualified deferred compensation plan subject to Section 409A?

A bonus life insurance or annuity plan uses a life insurance policy or annuity contract owned by the service provider to receive annual current bonus compensation contributions from the service recipient as a substitute for an unsecured and unfunded deferred compensation plan subject to Section 409A. This type of plan is commonly used in place of an employer-paid SERP by closely held businesses and tax-exempt entities.

The primary advantage of this type of plan is that increases in cash value are not subject to federal income tax until distribution. The owner can take pre-death distributions of cash value accumulated under a life insurance policy free of income tax to the extent of premiums paid, or borrow against the cash value without incurring income tax liability if the policy is maintained in force until the death of the insured. Proceeds payable on death are not subject to income tax and with appropriate planning can also be exempt from federal estate tax.

Distributions from an annuity after the annuity starting date are treated as pro rata from contributions and income; the part treated as contributions is not subject to income tax on receipt, and the part treated as income is subject to income tax at ordinary rates. However, proceeds of surrender before the annuity starting date are treated as income first and subject to tax at ordinary rates. On death of the annuitant, the annuity is treated as income in respect of a decedent for federal income and estate tax purposes.

In addition, annuities and especially life insurance can be protected from the creditors of the service recipient. Because the policy is not owned by the service recipient, it will not be subject to claims of its creditors. The laws of the service provider's state of residence govern the extent of the exemption from the service provider's creditors.

In addition, the bonus payment will be deductible by the service recipient in the year paid or accrued because it is current compensation rather than deferred compensation.

Because the service provider is required to recognize income for the taxable year in which the bonus is paid, to make the service provider's tax cost roughly equivalent to that of a deferred compensation plan, the service recipient would be required to gross up the bonus to include the time value of the tax incurred for the taxable year in which the bonus is paid. This would make the bonus approach more expensive for the service provider than a nonqualified deferred compensation plan subject to Section 409A, but the cost would be roughly offset by the deduction the service provider receives for current payment of the compensation. Also, because the service provider does not own the life insurance or annuity policy, the service provider does not have the advantage of the golden handcuffs a nonqualified deferred compensation plan provides. A restricted bonus life insurance plan that requires forfeiture of the benefit and return of the service recipient's contributions under the policy may be subject to Section 83 and the rules governing split-dollar plans, which make annual increases in cash value currently taxable to the service provider.

Also, a binding agreement to pay annual bonus payments for a period of years into a life insurance or annuity policy, a common practice prior to the effective date of Section 409A, constitutes a nonqualified deferred compensation plan subject to Section 409A. Even an annual compensation bonus can be subject to Section 409A if it is not paid within 2½ months after the end of the appropriate taxable year and therefore eligible for treatment as current compensation. Moreover, generally speaking, the arrangement will be subject to Section 409A if the service recipient continues to pay annual contributions into the policy after the service provider's separation from service, since post-employment payments are generally treated as deferred compensation (not for current services rendered) for purposes of Section 409A.

Citation: Consider a series of annual cash bonuses under Treasury Regulation Section 1.409A-1(b)(4)(i).

Q.82. Is a key person life insurance policy owned by the service recipient subject to Section 409A?

No. If a life insurance policy on the life of a service provider is owned and payable only to the service recipient upon the death of the participant, the policy is not subject to Section 409A. Such an arrangement is not a compensation arrangement at all, but rather a way for the service recipient to fund various potential costs and losses incident to the death of the insured, or to fund a buy-out of the interest of the insured in the service recipient's business.

Any other arrangement involving a life insurance policy may be subject to Section 409A. (See **Q. 79, Q. 80,** and **Q. 81.**) Also, Code Sections 101(j) and 6039I provide rules governing issuance, placement and reporting of employer-owned life insurance to obtain tax-free treatment of death proceeds under employer-owned life insurance, independent of Section 409A.

Citation: *See generally* Treasury Regulation Section 1.409A-1(a)(1), (b) and (c); Notice 2007-34, 2007-17 I.R.B., 4-23-2007.

FOREIGN PLANS

Q.83. Does Section 409A apply to deferred compensation attributable to services rendered outside the United States?

As with domestic nonqualified deferred compensation plans, foreign deferred compensation arrangements are subject to Section 409A, subject to specified exceptions. In the absence of an exception, Section 409A applies to the global income of U.S. citizens and resident aliens working abroad and also to U.S. source income of non-resident aliens.

The following deferred compensation arrangements are not subject to Section 409A:

- Foreign social security arrangements.

- Non-elective deferrals of foreign earned income, plus earnings thereon, under a broad-based foreign retirement plan or a plan under which substantially all participants are bona fide residents of a U.S. possession, so long as the service provider is not eligible to participate in a U.S. qualified employer plan. If the service provider is a U.S. citizen or lawful permanent resident, the exemption applies only to the extent that the non-elective deferrals would not exceed the limitations on benefits and contributions set forth in Sections 415(b) and (c) if the plan were a U.S. qualified plan.

  These exclusions apply even if the same plan also provides for elective deferrals and whether the plan sponsor is a U.S. or foreign employer.

- Payments pursuant to tax equalization agreements, so long as payment occurs by the end of the second full taxable year following the deadline for filing the service provider's U.S. or foreign income tax return for the year at issue (or if no foreign tax return is required, the due date of the foreign tax payment), whichever is later.

  In the alternative, these payments may be subject to the rules on tax gross-ups, audits or litigation settlements.

- Compensation excludable from income under U.S. tax law at the time it was earned or was no longer subject to a substantial risk of forfeiture pursuant to a tax treaty or convention entered into by the U.S. and a foreign country, plus earnings thereon.

- Compensation excludable from income under U.S. tax law at the time it was earned or was no longer subject to a substantial risk of forfeiture, plus earnings thereon, under the following Code provisions:

  - The service provider was a nonresident alien and the compensation would have been excludable as non-U.S. source income under Code Section 872.

  - The service provider was a U.S. citizen or resident living abroad and the compensation would have been excludable as foreign earned income under Code Section 911, to the extent that the total amount of current and deferred compensation for a year do not exceed the limit imposed by Section 911 for the year.

  - The service provider was either not a U.S. citizen or was a dual citizen of the U.S. and the Republic of the Philippines and was employed by a foreign government or international organization, and the compensation would have been excludable under Code Section 893.

  - The service provider was a resident of Guam, American Samoa, the Northern Mariana Islands or Puerto Rico and the compensation would have been excludable under Code Section 931 or 933.

- Elective deferrals of U.S.-source income by a non-resident alien under a foreign plan maintained by a foreign plan sponsor, up to the Section 402(g) limitation for the year, plus earnings thereon.

- Voluntary and involuntary foreign separation agreements, if payment is required by the foreign jurisdiction and payment is only from foreign-earned income sources in that jurisdiction.

- Section 402(b)-funded foreign arrangements.

Citation: ***See generally*** **Treasury Regulation Section 1.409A-1(b)(8) (i)-(iv).**

LIMITATIONS ON LINKING PLANS

Q.84. May a nonqualified deferred compensation plan that is an excess plan be linked to and controlled by a qualified retirement plan?

Generally, elections with respect to the time and form of distribution under an excess plan that provides benefits that could have been provided under a tax-qualified retirement plan but for the limits imposed by the Code on benefits, contributions and covered compensation cannot be linked to the underlying tax-qualified plan.

However, changes in a tax-qualified retirement plan required by the Code or other applicable law that results in an increase or decrease in the amounts accrued under an excess plan subject to Section 409A will not cause a prohibited deferral or acceleration under the excess plan so long as the changes do not otherwise change the time or form of payment under the excess plan; and the increase or decrease does not exceed the increase or decrease in the amount deferred under the underlying tax-qualified plan. The same rule applies to changes in the amount accrued under the excess plan by reason of:

- Action or inaction by a participant to elect to receive a subsidized or ancillary benefit under the qualified plan.
- Action or inaction by a participant with respect to making or adjusting elective deferrals and other participant pre-tax contributions under the qualified plan, provided that such action or inaction does not result in an increase or decrease of the participant's deferrals in excess of the Code Section 402(g)(1)(B) limit ($16,500 in 2010) plus the catch-up limit under Section 414(v) ($5,500 for 2010 for participants ages 50 or older) under the plan subject to Section 409A for a plan year.
- Action or inaction with regard to elective deferrals, other participant pre-tax and after-tax contributions under the tax-qualified plan that has an effect on the amounts credited as matching or other similar contingent amounts under plans subject to Section 409A, provided that any such matching or contingent amounts never exceed 100% of the amounts that would be provided under the qualified plan but for any qualified plan limitations on such contribution amounts.
- An amendment that adds or removes a subsidized or ancillary benefit, or that freezes or limits benefit accruals under the tax-qualified plan.

Also, a mere change of form of payment from one type of annuity to another actuarially equivalent annuity that starts at the same time is not subject to the prohibition against accelerations and the requirements of the subsequent election rule. (See **Q. 54.**) This allows a participant to change an annuity form of payment under the excess plan to match the form of payment selected under the tax-qualified plan without delaying distribution by five years.

Citation: Treasury Regulation Section 1.409A-2(b)(2)(ii)(A).

Q.85. Can the benefits from one nonqualified plan be offset against the benefits of another nonqualified plan?

Offsetting the benefits of one nonqualified plan against the benefits of another nonqualified plan will generally result in a Section 409A violation unless the two plans have identical payment provisions. If amounts payable under one nonqualified plan affect amounts payable under another, and if the two plans provide for different times and forms of payment, increasing or decreasing benefits under one plan may result in an acceleration or deferral of nonqualified benefits. For example, if an employer maintains a nonqualified account balance plan that provides that all benefits will be payable in a lump sum upon separation from service, plus a second account balance plan that pays benefits in 10 equal installments upon separation from service, and if the amount of the service provider's account balance under the first plan is offset by the amount of the service provider's account balance under the second plan, then an increase in benefits under the second plan will result in a deferral of the benefits that would otherwise have been paid in a lump sum under the first plan.

Citation: Annotated Regulations documenting the comments of William Schmidt at the ALI-ABA conference held on June 21, 2007 ("If you have two nonqualified plans that are linked together, you may have a problem"), and the comments of Daniel Hogans at the ALI-ABA conference held on May 21, 2007 ("If you have offsets between two nonqualified plans, you better make sure both those plans have identical payment provisions; otherwise you've blown yourself up"), reproduced in bold letters immediately following Treasury Regulation Section 1.409A-1(c)(2)(i)(C)(2).

FUNDING

Q.86. Does Section 409A permit assets in a rabbi trust or other trust to be restricted to fund a nonqualified deferred compensation plan incident to a change in the employer's financial condition?

No. Under Section 409A's funding rules, this would cause a taxable transfer under Section 83. This taxable transfer will occur upon the earlier of the date when the assets are actually restricted to fund benefits of the plan or the date when the plan first provides that the assets will be so restricted.

If a plan has a financial trigger that provides for funding all deferrals, all amounts deferred under the plan will be treated as a taxable Section 83 transfer. If a plan has a financial trigger that provides for funding the deferrals of specified individuals, all deferrals of those individuals will be treated as taxable Section 83 transfers. Subsequent increases in values and earnings on the restricted assets will be treated as additional transfers of property subject to tax under Section 83.

Citation: *See generally* 26 USC Section 409A(b)(2); Conf. Report, pp. 514-15, 524. The Final 409A Regulations (and the predecessor proposed 409A regulations) did not provide guidance interpreting the funding rules of Section 409A, so we have little guidance on them as of the date of publication.

Q.87. Is a plan subject to Section 409A required to be funded?

No.

To defer recognition of income by the service provider, Code Sections 61 and 451 require that nonqualified deferred compensation plans be unfunded, unsecured promises to pay the amounts due at a future time. Section 409A does not change these requirements. Nonqualified deferred compensation plans designed to be exempt from the funding, benefit accrual and vesting rules that apply to tax-qualified plans must also be unfunded.

Employers commonly establish reserves from which to satisfy their obligations under plans subject to Section 409A. The employer receives no current income tax deduction for amounts set aside to informally fund such plan; the income tax deduction is only allowed when the participant takes the benefit payment into gross income.

Depending on the type of plan, a variety of informal funding options is available to employers, such as mutual funds, grantor trusts (commonly known as rabbi trusts) and business-owned life insurance policies. Because the employer retains ownership of these assets, earnings and capital gains are taxable to the employer in the year in which they are realized. Therefore, employers commonly find low turnover mutual funds and business-owned life insurance policies suitable funding methods.

The amount of any reserve appears on the employer's balance sheet, and gains and losses are reflected in the employer's income statement. Death benefits paid under a deferred compensation plan are income in respect of a decedent.

These tax and accounting results apply independent of Section 409A. The suitability of an investment for a reserve established by the employer is also independent of Section 409A; the decision is generally based on the type of entity (for-profit or tax-exempt), plan design and objectives, and the employer's financial considerations.

Citation: *See generally* Treasury Regulation Section 1.451-2 as to prior income tax law; 26 USC Section 409A(b)(2); Conf. Report. pp. 514-15, 524 as to 409A "funding" rules. There were no regulations interpreting the funding rules under Section 409A(b)(2) as of the date of publication. *See generally* Richey, Baier & Brody, The Nonqualified Deferred Compensation Plan Advisor, Plans under 409A, 4th Edition, National Underwriter Company, for detailed information on the various informal funding, tax, accounting, SEC, security techniques and many other issues as to nonqualified deferred compensation plans.

Q.88. May an employer use an offshore trust to hold assets acquired in connection with a nonqualified deferred compensation plan covered by Section 409A?

No. Informally funding deferred compensation with assets held in an offshore trust is a violation of Section 409A, unless the majority of the services connected with the plan are rendered offshore. The assets held in all such trusts previously in existence were required to be distributed or disassociated with the employer's deferred compensation obligation by December 31, 2007.

Citation: 26 USC Section 409A(b)(2) as amended by the Gulf Opportunity Zone Act of 2005 ("GOZA"). There were no regulations interpreting the funding rules under Section 409A(b)(2) as of the date of publication.

Q.89. May a nonqualified deferred compensation plan be informally funded through a rabbi trust while the plan sponsor maintains an underfunded tax-qualified defined benefit retirement plan?

Assets may not be set aside in a trust or other arrangement for purposes of paying nonqualified deferred compensation during any "restricted period" with respect to a single-employer defined benefit plan maintained by the employer. The term "restricted period" means:

- Any period during which the defined benefit plan is in "at-risk status" (beginning in 2011, a plan will be considered in "at-risk status" if it is less than 80% funded);

- Any period during which the plan sponsor is in bankruptcy proceedings under Title 11; or

- The 18-month period before the defined benefit plan is terminated if, as of such termination date, the plan is underfunded.

This rule became effective on August 17, 2006.

Citation: GOZA adding 26 USC Section 409A (b)(3), as added by the Pension Protection Act of 2006. There were no regulations interpreting the funding rules under Section 409A(b)(2) as of the date of publication.

ENFORCEMENT

Q.90. Can an employer obtain an IRS letter ruling that a deferred compensation plan satisfies the requirements of Section 409A?

In general, no. Historically, sponsors would occasionally request a favorable private letter ruling from the IRS with respect to the income tax consequences of a nonqualified deferred compensation plan at the outset, based upon the plan's documentation (under Rev. Proc. 71-19, 1971-1 CB 698, as amplified by Rev. Proc. 92-65, 1992-2 CB 428). However, the IRS maintains a no-ruling position with respect to most Section 409A issues, including the following:

- The income tax consequences of establishing, operating, or participating in a plan, including withholding tax compliance

- Whether or not a plan is subject to a totalization agreement or is a foreign-based retirement plan that might be exempt from Section 409A

- Whether or not a plan is a bona fide vacation leave, sick pay, or compensatory time plan that might be exempt from Section 409A

- Whether or not a plan provides for deferral of compensation within the meaning of Section 409A and therefore might be covered by Section 409A

- Whether or not an amount might qualify as a short-term deferral that might thereby be exempt from Section 409A

- Whether or not certain stock rights, foreign plans, and separation pay plans are subject to Section 409A

Therefore, service recipients must rely on the statute, legislative history, regulations (final and proposed) and other guidance released by the IRS to determine compliance with or exemption from the requirements of Section 409A, with advice from their own counsel and other tax professionals.

The IRS will now rule on estate and gift tax and FICA issues involving a nonqualified deferred compensation arrangement. It is possible that the IRS would consider issuing a private letter ruling regarding other nonqualified deferred compensation matters not involving Section 409A.

Even before enactment of Section 409A, there was no IRS-approved model nonqualified deferred compensation plan document or plan language, and the IRS has not suggested that any model document or language will be forthcoming with respect to plans subject to Section 409A or plans of tax-exempt employers subject to Sections 409A and 457(f).

Citation: Rev. Proc. 2010-3, 2010-1 I.R.B. 110 (12-31-2009), superseding Rev. Proc. 2009-3; *see also* Rev. Proc. 2008-61, 2008-42 I.R.B. (10-20-2008), amplifying Rev Proc. 2008-3, 2008-1 I.R.B. 110 and superseded by Rev. Proc. 2009-3.

Q.91. When will the IRS actively audit and enforce the requirements of Section 409A on covered plans?

The IRS is auditing and enforcing these requirements now. Plans subject to Section 409A have been required to be in documentary and operational compliance as of January 1, 2009. This new income tax regime for nonqualified deferred compensation, including the new income tax penalties, was effective January 1, 2005, except for amounts grandfathered under plans not materially modified after October 4, 2004. From January 1, 2005, through December 31, 2008, plans were required to operate in good faith compliance with what was then known about the requirements of Section 409A.

Citation: 26 USC Section 409A(a)(1)(B)(i)(II); 26 USC Section 409A(b)(4)(A)(ii).

Q.92. Does the service recipient have income tax reporting obligations with respect to amounts accrued by participants in its deferred compensation plans governed by Section 409A?

Although the law technically requires deferred amounts to be reported, these reporting obligations have been suspended indefinitely. Once this suspension has been lifted, however, the service recipient will be required to report deferred amounts either on Form W-2 (for employees) or Form 1099-MISC (for independent contractors) each year. For individual account plans, the service recipient will be required to report additions to the account each year. For employer nonaccount balance plans (SERPs and excess plans), the employer will be required to report the actuarial increase in value of the benefit, either year by year or at such later time as the amount is reasonably ascertainable within the meaning of Code Section 3121(v)(2).

For employees, deferred amounts includible in income as a result of a Section 409A violation are treated as wages reported in Box 1 and as Section 409A income reported in Box 12 of Form W-2 using code "Z." The amount includible in income is treated as supplemental wages subject to income tax withholding, but the employer has no duty to withhold based on the additional excise tax and interest imposed pursuant to Section 409A.

For independent contractors, taxable deferred compensation is reported in Box 7 and in Box 15b of Form 1099-MISC.

Citation: 26 USC Sections 6041(g)(1) and 6051(a)(13); 26 USC Section 3401(a) as to withholding; *see generally* Proposed Treasury Regulation Section 1.409A-4 as to valuation when taxation is required under 409A. The IRS has issued a series of interim items over the past years regarding reporting and withholding requirements, including the delay of the informational reporting requirements (Notice 2005-1; Notice 2005-94; Notice 2006-100; Notice 2007-89, and Notice 2008-115).

MITIGATION OF CONSEQUENCES OF SECTION 409A VIOLATIONS

Q.93. Are there ways to limit the negative tax consequences of documentary errors under Section 409A?

Yes. Notice 2010-6 provides rules for correcting certain documentary errors under Section 409A. Documentary failures not expressly addressed in the notice are not eligible for relief under this guidance.

The Notice provides for relief with respect to some common types of plan provision without requiring a plan amendment.

One potential error is the use of a provision for payment as soon as practical (or similar language) following a payment event, such as separation from service, change in control or disability. This could be a technical problem because it contains the embedded element of discretion as to the time of payment, which is prohibited by Section 409A. In such cases, the date of the payment event will be treated as the fixed date for payment required by Section 409A, and payment will be considered timely if payment occurs or begins by the later of the end of the calendar year in which the payment event occurs or 2½ months after the payment event.

Another potential error is the use of ambiguous terms, for example, reference to termination of employment rather than the technically correct separation from service defined in accordance with Section 409A. Such different usage does not constitute a breach of Section 409A so long as the term used in the plan is applied in a manner consistent with Section 409A. If the term is applied inconsistently with Section 409A, a documentation failure occurs, and the plan must be amended to comply with Section 409A.

Other errors in plan documentation must be corrected by plan amendment and, in some cases, recognition of current income by the service provider and payment of the 20% excise tax on the amount recognized. Only inadvertent errors are subject to correction, and the plan sponsor is required to correct all similar errors in all of its plans. Neither the plan sponsor nor the service provider can be under audit at the time of correction. Stock rights and other plans under which the amount or time of payment is linked to other qualified or nonqualified deferred compensation plans cannot be corrected this way, although they may be subject to correction if action is taken by December 31, 2011. Any plan amendment making such a correction is subject to special reporting requirements.

The following errors are subject to correction by plan amendment:

- Impermissible definition of separation from service, change in control or disability: Correct the provision, or in the case of disability only, remove disability as a payment event.
- Impermissible payment or commencement period longer than 90 days following a payment event: Correct the provision or remove the period for payment after the event.
- Impermissible provision for payment after service provider provides a required release, non-compete agreement, etc: Make the payment date independent of the date the service provider provides the release or provide a fixed date that gives ample time for the service provider to return the release.
- Impermissible payment events in a plan that contains both permissible and impermissible payment events: Remove the impermissible payment events. This relief is not available for impermissible payment events that include discretion on the part of either party.
- Impermissible payment events in a plan that contains only impermissible payment events: Replace the impermissible payment event with a provision for payment on the later of separation from service or the sixth anniversary of the correction.
- Impermissible discretion to change a payment schedule: Remove the impermissible provision and revert to the default time and form of payment provided for in the plan, or if the plan does not contain a default, revert to the form with the latest payment date.
- Impermissible discretion to accelerate payment: Remove the discretion.
- Impermissible reimbursements or in-kind benefits: Amend to comply with Section 409A.
- Failure to include six-month delay in payment for specified employees who separate from service with a publicly held corporation: Add a provision that delays payment until the later of 18 months after correction or six months after separation.
- Impermissible initial deferral elections: Remove the provision. If the provision has been applied with respect to a plan participant, correct resulting operational failures under Notice 2009-113.
- Impermissible provision for payment of commissions after the service recipient's receipt of payments from a third party: Amend the provision to comply with the requirements of Section 409A not later than December 31, 2011; correct operational failures under Notice 2009-113.

Citation: Notice 2010-6, 2010-3 I.R.B. 275 (1-6-2010).

Q.94. Are there ways to limit the negative tax consequences of operational errors under Section 409A?

Yes. Notice 2008-113 provides rules for correcting certain operational failures under Section 409A. Operational failures not expressly addressed in the Notice are not eligible for relief under this guidance.

To be eligible for relief under this guidance, all of the following criteria must be met:

- The error is of a type described in the Notice.
- The error was inadvertent and unintentional.
- The employer or other service recipient has taken commercially reasonable steps to avoid recurrence of the error.
- The income tax return of the employee or other service provider for the year of error is not the subject of an IRS audit at the time of correction of the error.
- If the error involves a mistaken payment to the employee or other service provider, the payment did not coincide with a substantial financial downturn of the employer or other service recipient.

Relief under the Notice is available only for the following errors:

- Payment of nonqualified deferred compensation before the taxable year provided for payment under the terms of the plan (other than violations of the required six-month delay for "specified employees" of publicly traded entities)
- Payment of nonqualified deferred compensation during the taxable year provided for payment under the terms of the plan, but more than 30 days before the date specified for payment
- Payment of nonqualified deferred compensation to a "specified employee" of a publicly traded entity within the six-month period following the employee's separation from service
- Deferral of a greater or smaller amount of compensation than provided for under the terms of the plan
- Issuance of a stock right treated as deferred compensation because the exercise price is less than fair market value on the date of grant

The Notice specifies particular correction methods for the each type of error, generally including reversal of the error. For example, in the case of early distribution, the employee or other service provider must repay the amount distributed plus earnings, and the employer or other service recipient must make a subsequent distribution at the time provided for in the plan. In addition, the employer or other service recipient must report the error on the affected employee or other service recipient's Form W-2 or 1099, corrected if necessary, and withhold income tax on the amount recognized as income in connection with the correction (but not the 20% excise tax).

To obtain full relief, correction must occur no later than the year following the year in which the error occurred. However, if the employee or other service provider is an "insider," correction must occur in the same year as the error to obtain full relief. Who is an insider is determined under the Securities and Exchange Commission rules that apply to public companies, without regard to whether the company is public. Generally insiders are directors, officers and beneficial owners of more than 10% of any class of equity security of the employer or other service recipient. If the service recipient is not a corporation, these rules are applied by analogy.

Limited relief is available for errors involving small amounts in cases of failure to defer the right amount, payment to a specified employee within six months of separation from service and payment in the appropriate taxable year, but more than 30 days before the specified date. The error cannot involve more than the Section 402(g) limit on employee deferrals under a 401(k) plan for the year of error ($16,500 for 2010), and all amounts affected by similar errors with respect to the same employee or other service provider in all plans of the same type must be aggregated for this purpose. If an error meeting these standards is corrected by the end of the second taxable year following the taxable year in which the error occurred, the income tax and 20% penalty tax due under Section 409A are imposed only on the amount involved in the error, and the interest component of the tax is waived.

Other covered errors that do not involve a stock right and are corrected by the end of the second full taxable year following the taxable year of the error are entitled to the same relief as that available for errors involving small amounts.

Limited transition relief available for errors that occurred before 2008 expired in 2009.

Citation: *See generally* IRS Notice 2008-113, 2008-51 I.R.B. 1305, 12-22-2008; Berglund, Van Fleet, and Wolff, Section 409A in Action, BNA's Executive Compensation Library on the Web, 10-16-2009; for an excellent article that persuasively argues that operational errors should be correctable (particularly in the year of failure) for purposes of Section 409A even if the requirements of Notice 2008-113 cannot be met, *see also* Barker and O'Brien, 409A Failures: Correcting With and Without Notice 2008-113, Tax Notes August 10, 2009 at 557.

EFFECTIVE DATES

Q.95. What was the statutory effective date of Section 409A?

By its terms, Section 409A applies generally on and after January 1, 2005. However, deferred amounts to which the service provider had a legally binding right and that were both earned and vested as of December 31, 2004, and earnings on such amounts under plans in existence on October 3, 2004, are not subject to Section 409A unless there is a material modification of the plan provisions governing those amounts after October 3, 2004. Amounts that were not both earned and vested as of December 31, 2004, are not grandfathered and therefore are subject to Section 409A, even if they were accrued under a plan which includes amounts that are grandfathered.

Citation: Treasury Regulation Section 1.409A-6(a)(1)(i).

Q.96. When is a grandfathered plan considered to have been materially modified?

Deferred amounts that were both earned and vested as of December 31, 2004, and subsequent earnings on those amounts are eligible for grandfathering, so long as the plan under which they are subject is not materially modified after October 3, 2004. (See **Q. 95.**) For this purpose, material modification means the addition of a material benefit or right or the material enhancement of a benefit or right but not the exercise or reduction of an existing benefit, right or feature. For example, accelerated vesting of amounts accrued but not vested as of October 3, 2004, even if such accelerated vesting occurred before January 1, 2005, would constitute a material modification. Addition of a haircut provision would also be treated as a material modification, but removal of a haircut provision would not. Exercise of discretion permitted under the terms of a provision which was included in the plan on October 3, 2004, would not be treated as a material modification, but addition of a provision permitting the exercise of discretion would generally constitute a material modification. A plan amendment providing for distribution in the case of an unforeseeable emergency or for subsequent elections to change the time or form of payment would also be treated as a material improvement causing loss of grandfathered status.

The regulations list a number of modifications applicable to grandfathered plans that would *not* constitute material modifications for purposes of the grandfathering rules:

- Establishment of or contributions to a rabbi trust
- Amendment of a plan to require compliance with a domestic relations order with respect to payments to an individual other than the service provider
- Amendment of a plan providing payment in the form of a life annuity to permit an election between the existing life annuity form and other actuarially equivalent forms of annuity payments
- Amendment of a grandfathered plan to add a limited cash-out feature consistent with the limited cash-out feature allowed under a Section 409A-compliant plan. (See **Q. 29**.)
- Termination of a plan pursuant to the provisions of the plan
- Addition of additional notional investment options under an account balance plan to the extent that the new investment options are based on a predetermined actual investment (as defined in Treasury Regulation Section 31.3121(b)(2)-1(d)(2)) or a reasonable interest crediting rate.

If a plan is inadvertently materially modified in a manner that causes the loss of grandfathered treatment, grandfathered status may be preserved if the material modification is rescinded before the earlier of the last day of the calendar year in which the modification was made or before any new right is exercised (in the case of a material modification granting a discretionary right). For example, if an employer modifies the terms of a grandfathered plan on March 1 to allow an employee to elect a new change in the time or form of payment without realizing that such a change constitutes a material modification, and if the modification is rescinded on the following November 1, then the plan will not lose grandfathered treatment provided no change in the time or form of payment has been made before November 1.

At a practical level, grandfathered amounts must be identifiable to claim the protection of grandfathering. (See **Q. 97**.) If grandfathered amounts and amounts subject to Section 409A are held under a single plan document, care must be taken not to make an inadvertent material modification of the plan provisions governing the grandfathered amounts by plan amendment or restatement. Care must also be taken that the grandfathered assets remain subject to the prior plan rules in operation as well as form, such that any more favorable current rules are not inadvertently applied to the grandfathered amounts. To avoid such issues, many sponsors of deferred compensation plans froze the plan governing the grandfathered amounts and created a separate new plan designed to comply with the requirements of Section 409A for amounts accrued but not vested as of December 31, 2004, and subsequent deferrals.

Citation: *See generally* 26 USC Section 409A(D)(2)(B); Treasury Regulation Section 1.409A-6(a)(1)-(4); *see also* the American Jobs Creation Act of 2004, Section 885(d), and the American Jobs Creation Act of 2004 Conference Report pp. 526-7.

Q.97. How are amounts eligible for grandfathering determined?

Account Balance Plans.

The amount of compensation that is considered grandfathered under a nonqualified deferred compensation plan that is an account balance plan equals the portion of the service provider's account balance as of December 31, 2004, which was earned and vested as of December 31, 2004, plus earnings on that portion of the account balance. For this purpose, a right to earnings that is subject to either a substantial risk of forfeiture or a requirement to perform further services is not treated as earnings on the grandfathered amount, but a separate right to compensation.

Example. On December 31, 2004, an executive has a fully vested right to a nonqualified deferred compensation account balance of $100,000. Interest on the account balance is credited based on the five-year Treasury rate. However, for those individuals who continue employment until reaching age 55 with 10 years of service, interest is retroactively recalculated based upon the five-year Treasury rate plus one percent. As of December 31, 2004, the executive is only age 45. The amount of the executive's grandfathered compensation is $100,000 plus interest at the five-year Treasury rate. If the executive works until age 55 and thereby earns the right to an additional one percent annual interest, that additional interest will not be considered as part of the grandfathered arrangement because the right to such earnings was subject to a substantial risk of forfeiture as of December 31, 2004 (*i.e.*, the requirement that the executive work another 10 years in order to earn the right to such additional interest). Thus, the additional interest constitutes deferred compensation that is subject to the requirements of Section 409A.

Nonaccount Balance Plans.

The amount of grandfathered compensation under a nonqualified deferred compensation plan that is a nonaccount balance plan equals the present value of the amount to which the service provider would have been entitled under the plan if the service provider voluntarily terminated employment without cause on December 31, 2004, and received payment of the benefits available from the plan on the earliest possible date allowed under the plan in the form of benefit with the greatest value. This grandfathered amount may increase after December 31, 2004, by use of the interest rate used to determine the present value of the benefit as of December 31, 2004. In addition, the present value of the benefit may increase as a result of the service provider's survivorship during the year based on the mortality assumptions used to calculate the present value of the grandfathered benefit. However, an increase in the potential benefits due to an increase in compensation under a final average pay plan or qualification for an early retirement subsidy after December 31, 2004, does not constitute earnings on amounts deferred under the plan before January 1, 2005, and is not grandfathered.

Citation: Treasury Regulation Section 1.409A-6(a)(3).

Q.98. Are grandfathered amounts subject to any restrictions on distribution?

Yes. Although grandfathered plans need not satisfy the requirements of Section 409A, they must continue to satisfy the constructive receipt and other income tax rules in effect prior to the effective date of Section 409A and the governing plan provisions (**Q. 44**).

Citation: 26 U.S.C. Section 409A(c).

Q.99. What was the effective date for actual compliance with Section 409A?

Because of the complexity of the subject matter, it took a long time to develop the regulatory framework for enforcement of Section 409A. Final regulations were published in April 2007 and, after a series of extensions, became generally applicable for service providers' taxable years beginning on or after January 1, 2009, with respect to both documentary and operational compliance. However, Notice 2010-6 permits retroactive correction of documentary errors through December 31, 2010, effective as of January 1, 2009. (See **Q. 93**.)

Citation: IRS Notice 2007-86 extending Treasury Regulation Section 1.409A-6(b) that originally set January 1, 2008, as the effective date; *see also* "Dates Section," Preamble to the Final 409A Regulations.

Q.100. What were the standards for compliance with Section 409A for the transition period between the statutory effective date, January 1, 2005, and December 31, 2008?

Section 409A became applicable by its terms as of January 1, 2005. However final regulations were not issued until 2007 and the operational effective date was extended on a year-to-year basis to January 1, 2009. In the intervening transition period, taxpayers were required to operate in good faith compliance with Section 409A and IRS guidance issued during the transition period, including proposed and final regulations and IRS notices. A plan's good faith compliance during the transition period need not be documented in the plan, but good faith compliance must be demonstrable on audit, which requires at the least adequate documentation of the manner in which the plan was administered.

Citation: Notices 2005-1, 2005-1 C.B. 274, 2007-78, 2007-41 I.R.B. 780, Notice 2007-100, 2007-52 I.R.B. 1243 (12-31-2007); Preamble to the 409A Regulations.

Exhibit 1

Summary Process for Creating Compensation and Benefit Plans in Connection With Code § 409A

Suggested Seven-Step Summary Process for Approaching Compensation and Benefit Plans and Section 409A

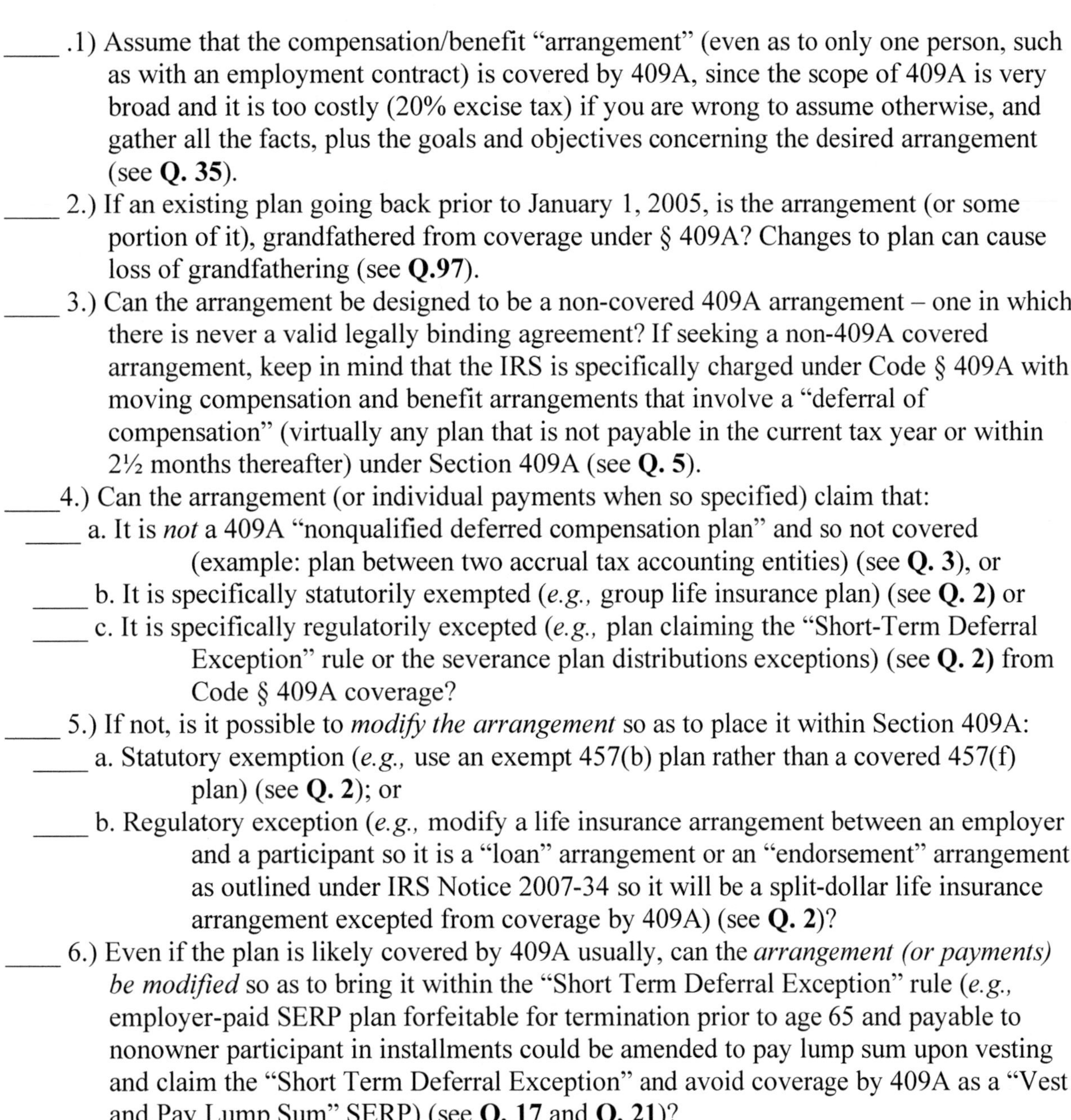

____ .1) Assume that the compensation/benefit "arrangement" (even as to only one person, such as with an employment contract) is covered by 409A, since the scope of 409A is very broad and it is too costly (20% excise tax) if you are wrong to assume otherwise, and gather all the facts, plus the goals and objectives concerning the desired arrangement (see **Q. 35**).

____ 2.) If an existing plan going back prior to January 1, 2005, is the arrangement (or some portion of it), grandfathered from coverage under § 409A? Changes to plan can cause loss of grandfathering (see **Q.97**).

____ 3.) Can the arrangement be designed to be a non-covered 409A arrangement – one in which there is never a valid legally binding agreement? If seeking a non-409A covered arrangement, keep in mind that the IRS is specifically charged under Code § 409A with moving compensation and benefit arrangements that involve a "deferral of compensation" (virtually any plan that is not payable in the current tax year or within 2½ months thereafter) under Section 409A (see **Q. 5**).

____4.) Can the arrangement (or individual payments when so specified) claim that:

____ a. It is *not* a 409A "nonqualified deferred compensation plan" and so not covered (example: plan between two accrual tax accounting entities) (see **Q. 3**), or

____ b. It is specifically statutorily exempted (*e.g.,* group life insurance plan) (see **Q. 2)** or

____ c. It is specifically regulatorily excepted (*e.g.,* plan claiming the "Short-Term Deferral Exception" rule or the severance plan distributions exceptions) (see **Q. 2)** from Code § 409A coverage?

____ 5.) If not, is it possible to *modify the arrangement* so as to place it within Section 409A:

____ a. Statutory exemption (*e.g.,* use an exempt 457(b) plan rather than a covered 457(f) plan) (see **Q. 2**); or

____ b. Regulatory exception (*e.g.,* modify a life insurance arrangement between an employer and a participant so it is a "loan" arrangement or an "endorsement" arrangement as outlined under IRS Notice 2007-34 so it will be a split-dollar life insurance arrangement excepted from coverage by 409A) (see **Q. 2**)?

____ 6.) Even if the plan is likely covered by 409A usually, can the *arrangement (or payments) be modified* so as to bring it within the "Short Term Deferral Exception" rule (*e.g.,* employer-paid SERP plan forfeitable for termination prior to age 65 and payable to nonowner participant in installments could be amended to pay lump sum upon vesting and claim the "Short Term Deferral Exception" and avoid coverage by 409A as a "Vest and Pay Lump Sum" SERP) (see **Q. 17** and **Q. 21**)?

____ 7.) If the plan *cannot* escape coverage of Section 409A under any of the prior approaches, make certain that the arrangement (see **Q. 1**) conforms to the requirements of 409A "detail requirements" in both (see **Q. 11**):

____ a. Form (documentation) using Notice 2010-6 as a checklist, and

____ b. Operation (administration) - by hiring a TPA with special record-keeping capability and processes for administering a nonqualified deferred compensation plans covered by Code § 409A in a compliant fashion.

Exhibit 2

Section 409A "Performance-Based Compensation" Quick Qualification Checklist

The following questions *must all* receive a "YES" answer (except for question #6) for compensation to qualify as "performance-based compensation" and claim the special participant election treatment under the Section 409A provision that permits the final irrevocable deferral election to be made 6 months prior to the end of the bonus performance period.

Question #6 sorts out the portion of compensation (if any) that does not qualify for the special election opportunity because of the Section 409A requirement that the bonus amounts be nonascertainable at the time of the deferral election. Sorting the nonascertainable from the ascertainable amounts may require some review.

1.) Were the requirements to receive the incentive compensation communicated in writing to the participants not later than at least 90 days into the performance year? Yes __ No __

2.) Does the performance plan period and each participant's active participation run for a sequence of 12 full calendar months (quarterly performance periods, etc., do not qualify)? Yes __ No __

3.) Is this the only elective account balance plan that the eligible employee(s) currently participate in? Yes __ No __

4.) Is the plan based upon communicated quantitative and qualitative factors rather than being wholly discretionary? Yes __ No ___

5.) Will the deferral elections be made not later than 6 full calendar months prior to the end of the performance period (prior to July 1 for calendar year performance plans)? Yes __ No __

6.) What part of the compensation is NOT readily ascertainable (calculable and substantially certain to be paid) as of the election deadline (only the portion of bonus that is not yet ascertainable as of the date may qualify for the special election if other factors met)?

__ All of the bonus (up to 100% election)
__% of total

Exhibit 3

SPECIMEN QUESTIONNAIRE FOR CODE § 409A FINANCIAL HARDSHIP DISTRIBUTION REQUEST

PARTICIPANT REQUEST:

Plan Name: ____

I wish to request an "unforeseen emergency" distribution from the above plan by the:

[ ] Distribution of the salary deferrals under my current Deferral Election Form in the total "need" amount shown below by the termination of the deferral of these amounts from my salary payroll for the balance of the current Plan Year.

[ ] Distribution of my vested account balance under the Plan to address the total "need" amount shown below (or my total account as necessary), since my total need exceeds the amount generated by the elimination of my deferral for the Plan Year.

I request distribution based upon the following information herein provided. I understand that I am only entitled to this emergency distribution subject to certain specific requirements, conditions and limitations as outlined by Internal Revenue Code Section 409A and the guidance thereto. I affirm and certify that the information here provided is true and correct to the best of my knowledge as of the date hereafter noted. I agree to provide any other or additional information or documentation as may be requested to establish the nature and extent of my financial hardship for purposes of this distribution in order to establish both my eligibility for and allowable need amount under Section 409A.

I. Participant Information-

1. Name:____
2. Address:_______________________________, ___________, ____, _____

   (Street Address) (City) (State) (ZIP)
3. Employee Identification Code: ____________________
4. Phone: ( )____-______ Email: ______________________ Fax: ______________

II. W-4 Information-

This distribution, if made, is subject to Federal Withholding Tax. The amount of tax withheld will depend on the W-4 you have currently filed with the company. Your W-4 will also govern the amount of allowable tax we can distribute in addition to your any need amount. It is suggested that 15 to 30% be withheld to cover additional taxes caused by this distribution. If you wish the withholding to be larger than that based upon your current W-4 (by filing a special W-4) for this distribution, please indicate below:

Larger withholding desired? Yes__ No __

III. Hardship Information (Check and complete as appropriate)

1. The nature of my financial hardship was unforeseeable and not under my control.

   Yes___ No ___

2. The nature of my current financial situation constitutes a real financial emergency that threatens to cause me great financial hardship or detriment if not relieved by a complete termination of my deferrals and/or immediate distribution from my account.

Yes ___ No ___

3. The nature of my financial hardship is as follows:

   a. A sudden or unexpected illness or accident (me / spouse / dependent) causing loss of income (by loss of employment, disability) and/or unexpected medical expenses related to the illness or accident _____ **;or**

   b. A loss of my property (for example, home, auto) due to an unforeseen casualty loss (for example, fire, earthquake, flood) _____ **;or**

   c. Another extraordinary and financial loss or emergency beyond my control as follows (Detail the nature of the situation. For example, death, loss of employment of spouse, reduction of living income by divorce, etc):

   ____

   ____.

4. The *magnitude of my financial emergency* in a lump sum is: $_____________

5. *Income* from all other readily available sources to apply to debt: $_____________

   (From regular income, insurance, liquid assets)

6. *Total amount of distribution needed* to relieve financial hardship:

   (#4 minus #5) **$ _____________**

7. The amount of expected income taxes on that amount is: $_____________

8. The total amount of the distribution accounting for taxes is: **$_____________**

9. The total amount in my Plan account as of __/__/____ is: $ _____________

10. Total amount available from cessation of my remaining deferral

    this calendar Plan Year beginning as of __/__/____ is: $_____________

Submission Date: ____/____/_____

Participant Name: ____

Participant Signature (required):______________________________________

____

Due to the time necessary to evaluate an "Unforeseen Emergency" distribution and to process a cessation of deferral or surrender of an account under the Plan, payment should not be expected for a minimum of 2 to 4 weeks from receipt of completed paperwork by the Plan Administrator.

Administrator's Review Checklist (for use by the Company to determine action):

1.) Event is a qualified unforeseeable emergency under 409A? ( ) *YES* ( ) *NO* (If "NO", ***no*** *distribution may be made by reason of Code Section 409A limitations that includes a 20% excise tax penalty for a violation).*

2.) If eligible, other financial resources are ( ) wholly unavailable; and/or ( ) are inadequate to the extent of $_____________ lump sum.

3.) The financial emergency can be resolved by:

( ) Distribution by cessation of the Participant's salary deferrals for the balance of the calendar year

( ) Distribution from the participant's account the lump sum of $_______________, plus taxes in the amount of $_________________.

( ) Both

4.) The Company will notify the participant that:

( ) the request for distribution is denied because the event is NOT a qualified "unforeseeable emergency" under 409A.

( ) the event is a qualified unforeseeable emergency, but no distribution can be made because the participant has sufficient other resources that can be used to meet the emergency

( ) the event qualifies as an "unforeseeable emergency"; that other resources are inadequate to meet the financial emergency to the extent of $_______________; and a distribution will be made-

( ) by cessation of the participant's salary deferral for the balance of the calendar year beginning __/__/____ amounting to $_______________ total.

( ) from the participant's plan account of $__________________, plus an amount for taxes on that distribution of $_________________, which amount does not exceed the current available vested balance.

( ) from the participant's entire available account balance of $_______________, which is less than the participant's total financial "need", including taxes on that "need" amount.

Approved for the following total plan distribution: $_________________Company Official:
______________________________ Date: _____________, 20_Company Official's Signature:
____

Disapproved for any plan distribution.

Company Official: ________________________________ Date: ____________, 20__

Company Official's Signature: ____

DISCLAIMER

THIS FORM IS A SPECIMEN OF THE TYPE OF FORM TO BE USED IN CONNECTION WITH A PARTICIPANT'S REQUEST FOR DISTRIBUTION OF BENEFITS FROM A NONQUALIFIED DEFERRED COMPENSATION PLAN BY REASON OF AN "UNFORSEEABLE EMERGENCY".

Exhibit 4

DOMESTIC RELATIONS ORDER

Nonqualified Deferred Compensation Plan Under Section 409A

Specimen for Review of Counsel Only

_____________________ is a participant in the______________________________ (Plan), which is a nonqualified defined contribution deferred compensation plan, and is not subject to a Qualified Domestic Relations Order under 414(p) because it is not a qualified plan under 414(p), but an ERISA exempt unfunded plan for a select group of executives and highly compensated under ERISA, and thereby has no "plan assets". However, the plan is subject to Treas. Reg. Section 1.409A-3(i)(3), allowing for splitting and distribution of a nonqualified plan account. On_________________________, this matter was before the Court, and the Court having heard evidence and the Findings of Fact, Conclusions of Law and Judgment of Divorce having been filed, and certain provisions therein having awarded ____an interest in ______________________________'s vested accrued benefit promise in the Plan, and this Order being necessary to carry forth such provisions:

IT IS ORDERED that the following disposition be made:

Upon receipt of a certified copy of this judgment and if the above-referenced nonqualified deferred compensation plan so allows, the administrator(s) of the Plan, which is______________________________, the nonqualified plan's sponsor who is the Participant's employer, shall direct its record keeper of the Plan's hypothetical accounts, McCamish Systems LLC, to divide the hypothetical account(s) of _________________, into two (2) parts: one for _______________, consisting of [one-half] of each specific account as of ____________ [date] after adjustments for earnings, appreciation, and contributions; the remaining balance in each specific account shall be retained for ______________________. No credit shall be made to the [Respondent's] account with respect to contributions made by the [Petitioner] or by the employer or with respect to any other crediting to each specific account in the plan after __________ [date].

And, if the plan so allows, the plan administrator(s), shall distribute to [Respondent] in a single total lump-sum, from any sources that the plan administrator shall determine appropriate for this unsecured promise-to-pay plan, an amount equal to the value of her [his] portion of the hypothetical account(s) maintained by McCamish Systems LLC, as outlined above. Receipt of a certified copy of this judgment by the plan administrator(s) shall fulfill any and all requirements of the Plan as to necessary notice and request by [Respondent] for a distribution from the Plan in consequence of a separation of marital property between the [Petitioner] and [Respondent], and protect the Plan Sponsor, the Plan and the other Plan participants from any adverse Federal or State (local) income tax consequences, especially under Section 409A, based upon compliance with this Order.

Distribution to [Respondent] shall be made as soon as administratively possible, as permitted by IRC Reg. § 1.409A-3(j)(4)(ii), but in compliance with IRC § 409A generally, and IRC Reg. § 1.409A-2 specifically, and this distribution shall occur not later than would a distribution to the participant in the Plan under a specified future date election, except that this distribution shall not be subject to any application of the "6- month delay rule" under IRC § 409A and the regulations thereto as provided for domestic relations orders on 409A nonqualified deferred compensation plans.

This provision is designed to meet the definition of a Qualified Domestic Relations Order under IRC §414(p) *only to the extent* necessary to satisfy the requirements for a domestic relations order under IRC § 409A and the regulations thereto, and nothing in this order is intended to suggest that the Plan is either a funded plan for ERISA (one with Plan assets) or income tax purposes (a secured plan). The parallel requisites for this Order are fulfilled in the following provisions of this instrument.

The name, address, and social security number of the participant [the Petitioner] are as follows:

____

____

____

The name, address, and social security number of the alternate payee [the Respondent] are as follows:

____

____

____

The [Respondent's] interest shall be determined by taking [one-half] of the value of each hypothetical Plan account as of _______________ [date]. The benefit for the [Petitioner] shall be the balance of each hypothetical Plan account. The [Respondent's] interest also shall include any interest, dividends, or other proceeds attributable to [Respondent's] share up to the date the specific account(s) is/are actually divided. In addition, the [Respondent] shall be treated as a surviving spouse for the full value of her [his] share until the hypothetical account(s) actually is/are divided.

The number of payments required is [one (1)] from the Plan.

The name of the Nonqualified Deferred Compensation Plan (Plan) for which this order applies is:

____.

The terms and provisions of this Order are not to be construed to:

Require a plan to provide any type or form of benefit or any option (with the exception of the payment to the [Respondent] as provided above) not otherwise provided under the plan;
Require a plan to provide increased benefits (determined on the basis of actuarial value); or
Require the payment of benefits to the [Respondent], which are required to be paid to another alternate payee under another order previously determined to apply to the Plan.

The [Respondent] shall have the duty to notify the plan administrator(s) in writing of any change in her [his] mailing address.
It is the intention of the court that the distribution by the Plan to the [Respondent] and the [Petitioner] shall be taxable on the income under the guidelines of IRS Rev. Rul. 2002-22.

Dated:______________________________

BY THE COURT:

Disclaimer

This document is for informational purposes only of the type of Domestic Relations Order used in connection with the division of martial property involving a nonqualified deferred compensation plan under Code Section 409A. It is provided as an aid to private legal counsel and should not be used except after proper consultation of legal counsel as to the party's particular circumstances.

Exhibit 5

Notice 2008-113

OPERATIONAL ERROR SUPER SUMMARY

FOR CORRECTION OF NON QUALIFIED RETIREMENT INCOME PLANS

(Excludes Correction for Stock Right Failure)

Exhibit 5

NOTICE 2008-113 Correction Process Summary. Do not use this summary as a substitute for the Notice or for a stock error.	Error Corrected in Same Tax Year	Error Corrected in the Following Tax Year <u>*Noninsiders Only*</u>	Error Corrected Before End of Second Tax Year (aggregate amounts *less than* 402(g)(1)(B) limit)	Error Corrected Before End of Second Tax Year (aggregate amounts *more than* 402(g)(1)(B) limit)
Under-Deferrals or Early Payment Wrong Year	* EE must repay amounts *Noninsiders:* No interest *Insiders:* AFR interest if amount exceeds 402(g)(1)(B) limit * No 20%; no penalty interest tax. * Account may be adjusted for earnings & losses. <u>*Citation:*</u> IV.A.	* EE must repay amounts with interest. * Original payment included in income in year paid: repayment is deductible in year paid (excluding interest); future payment included in income when paid. * Account may be adjusted retroactively for earnings & losses. <u>*Citation:*</u> V.B.	* EE does *not* repay. * Error amount only included in income; 20% but no penalty interest tax. * EE's W-2 / 1040 amended as to erroneous payment in year of error <u>*Citation:*</u> VI.B.	* EE must repay. *Noninsiders:* No interest. *Insiders:* Interest. * Error amount only included in income; 20% but no penalty interest tax. * EE's W-2 / 1040 amended as to erroneous payment in error year; no deduction for repayment; future payment then not included in income. Account may be retroactively adjusted for earnings & losses . <u>*Citation:*</u> VII.B.
Early Payment Correct Year (30 days prior or 6 month delay rule violations)	* EE must repay amounts. Subsequent payment to EE must be delayed by same number of days paid early. * No 20%; no penalty interest tax. * Account must *not* be adjusted for earnings but *may* be for losses. <u>*Citation:*</u> IV.B.	* EE must repay amounts. Subsequent payment to EE must be delayed by same number of days paid early. * Early payment included in income in year paid; future payment not included in income unless distributed in a subsequent year to repayment, in which event repayment is deductible. * No 20%; no penalty interest tax. * Account must *not* be adjusted for earnings but *may* be for losses. <u>*Citation:*</u> V.C.	* EE does not repay. * Error amount only included in income; 20% but no penalty interest tax. * EE's W-2 / 1040 amended as to erroneous payment in error year. <u>*Citation:*</u> VI.B.	* EE must repay. Subsequent payment to EE must be delayed by days paid early. * Error amount only included in income; 20% but no penalty interest tax. * EE's W-2 /1040 amended as to erroneous payment in error yr; no deduction for repayment; future payment then not included in income. Account may be retroactively adjusted for earnings & losses. <u>*Citation:*</u> VII.C.
Excess Deferral or Under Payment (late payments)	* ER must pay amounts ER may pay reasonable TVM interest. * Excess deferral/under payment * Under Payment corrected in same tax year *not* 409A violation so no tax is not 409A error and no relief. * No 20%; no penalty interest tax. * Account: Noninsiders: May be adjusted for earnings & losses. Insiders: Must be adjusted for earnings. <u>*Citation:*</u> IV.C.	* ER must pay excess amounts ER may *not* pay TVM interest. * ER corrective amounts included in income in year paid. * No 20%; no penalty interest tax. * Account must be adjusted retroactively for earnings & may adjust for losses back to error date. <u>*Citation:*</u> V.D. <u>*Note: V.D. does not clearly address Under Payment. Believed to be an oversight.*</u>	* ER must pay excess or under payment amounts. ER may not pay TVM interest. * Amount in error only included in income; 20% but no penalty interest tax. * EE's W-2 & 1040 amended to include payment. * Account: ER must distribute or forfeit earnings, but not retain; ER may reduce payment or ignore as to losses. <u>*Citation:*</u> VI.C.	* ER must pay excess or under payment amounts. ER may *not* pay TVM interest. * Error amount only included; 20% but no penalty interest tax. * EE's W-2 / 1040 amended for error year; no deduction for EE repayment; future payment then not included in income. * Account: ER must adjust for earnings & may adjust for losses. <u>*Citation:*</u> VII.D.

Index of Subjects